Traveling Calvary's Road

From Ash Wednesday Through Easter

Anne W. Anderson
Lynne Cragg
Howard Eshbaugh
Michelle Griep
Leonard V. Kalkwarf
William Luoma
Pamela D. Williams
Janice Bennett Wyatt

CSS Publishing Company, Inc., Lima, Ohio

TRAVELING CALVARY'S ROAD

Some scripture quotations are from the Good News Bible, in Today's English Version. Copyright © American Bible Society 1966, 1971, 1976. Used by permission.

Some scripture quotations are from the New Revised Standard Version of the Bible, copyright 1989 by the Division of Christian Education of the National Council of Churches of Christ in the USA. Used by permission.

Some scripture quotations are from the Revised Standard Version of the Bible, copyrighted 1946, 1952 ©, 1971, 1973, by the Division of Christian Education of the National Council of the Churches of Christ in the USA. Used by permission.

Some scripture quotations are from the Holy Bible, New International Version. Copyright © 1973, 1978, 1984 International Bible Society. Used by permission of Zondervan Bible Publishers. All rights reserved.

The sections written by William Luoma were taken from *God So Loved The World*, published by CSS Publishing Company, Inc., in 1986, ISBN: 0-89536-788-2.

The section written by Howard Eshbaugh was taken from *Hear The Good News*, published by CSS Publishing Company, Inc., in 1984, ISBN: 0-89536-656-8.

Your King Comes by Janice Bennett Wyatt was previous published by CSS Publishing Company, Inc., in 1992, ISBN 1-55673-406-9.

For more information about CSS Publishing Company resources, visit our website at www.csspub.com or email us at custserv@csspub.com or call (800) 241-4056.

Cover design by Nikki Nocera
ISBN-13: 979-0-7880-2431-2
ISBN-10: 0-7880-2431-0

PRINTED IN U.S.A.

Table Of Contents

Introduction

This anthology is designed to provide you with an abundance of services, dramas, monologues, and sermons to assist in your journey from Ash Wednesday through Easter.

Many of these allow you to integrate your own church's preference of style or hymns. One actually uses newspapers as a part of the service to make the worship more meaningful.

Traveling Calvary's Road is an important journey and we hope this serves you well.

Into The Wilderness

Ash Wednesday Service

Anne W. Anderson

Into The Wilderness

Introduction

Ash Wednesday begins the penitential season of Lent, the time the liturgical churches remember the forty days Jesus spent in the wilderness and the temptations he faced there. This service invites believers to follow Jesus into the wilderness and is in three parts. The first focuses on entering into the wilderness, the second describes the temptations we find there, and the third helps us to find victory over them.

Running Time

This runs thirty to sixty minutes depending on the length of the pastoral reflections and choice of optional music.

Worship Notes

This service is written for three readers, but can be adapted for as few as two or as many as six. Readers should represent, if possible, different ages (elementary age children through senior adults), genders, and ethnic backgrounds. The readings break sentences into fragments, each fragment being read by a different voice, to provide interest, to emphasize various words, and to convey a sense that the scriptures apply to each of us and are not limited to any one age or gender or nationality. Readers should practice together until the sentences flow smoothly. When words are repeated, each reader should vary the emphasis. For additional effect, position readers in different places throughout the sanctuary. Scriptures used are from the Good News Bible/Today's English Version.

The reflections can be offered by the pastoral staff or by lay leaders. These can be short reflections designed to lead the congregation into weekly Lenten studies, or they can be more fully developed homilies.

(Any announcements, welcoming statements, and opening prayers that are standard to a particular church should take place here before moving into the rest of the service.)

Invitation To Follow Jesus Into The Wilderness

All sing: "I have decided to follow Jesus (3x) / No turning back, no turning back"

Reader 1: A reading from the gospel of Mark, chapter 1, verses 9 through 13: Jesus came from Nazareth

Reader 2: in the province of Galilee

Reader 3: and was baptized by John in the Jordan.

Reader 1: As soon as Jesus came up out of the water,

Reader 2: he saw heaven opening

Reader 3: and the Spirit coming down on him like a dove.

Reader 1: And a voice came from heaven,

All: "You are my own dear Son. I am pleased with you."

Hymn: "As I Went Down In The River To Pray"

Alternate Hymn: "On Jordan's Banks The Baptist's Cry"

Reader 3: At once

Reader 2: at once, the Spirit made him

Readers 1 and 3: *made him*

Reader 2: made him go into the desert, where he stayed forty days, being tempted

Reader 3: *tempted*

Reader 1: tempted by Satan.

Reader 3: Wild animals were there also

Reader 1: but angels came and helped him.

(short pause)

Optional Hymn: "Forty Days And Forty Nights Thou Was Fasting In The Wild"

Reader 4: The first thing Jesus did after being baptized by John, being filled with the Holy Spirit, and being publicly recognized by God the Father as his "own dear Son," was not what we would expect. When we commission someone for a task, we expect him to go and do. Instead, Jesus retreated to the wilderness where he spent forty days. It is important for us to recognize that often our spiritual "highs" are followed by wilderness experiences and even testings. This evening [Today], we will look at each of the temptations Jesus faced during that forty-day period — temptations that we can expect to face during our walk with Jesus.

Reader 5: During some baptism services, the person being baptized renounces — for Jesus' sake — the world, the flesh, and the devil. These were the three temptations Jesus faced ... and are basically the same three we face.

The Temptations We Meet In The Wilderness

All sing: "Though none go with me, still I will follow (3x) / No turning back, no turning back"

Reader 1: A reading from the Gospel of Matthew, chapter 4, verses 2 through 4: After spending forty days

Reader 2: and nights

Reader 1: without food

Reader 3: Jesus was hungry. Then the Devil came to him and said

Reader 2: "If you are God's Son, order these stones to turn into bread."

Reader 1: But Jesus answered, "The scripture says:

All: 'Human beings cannot live on bread alone

Reader 3: but need every word

Reader 2: *every* word

Reader 1: every word that God

Reader 3: that *God*

Reader 2: that God speaks.' "

Pastoral Reflection on the temptations of the flesh [self vs. God] including those of the body (gluttony, lust), the soul (pride, frivolity), and the spirit (despair, heresy). Suggested scripture references: Jeremiah 17:9-10; Galatians 5:16—6:5; 1 Corinthians 9:24—10:23; Galatians 4:17—5:10; Romans 8; Ephesians 4:17—5:20.

Personal Reflection And Silent Prayer

Reader 2: A reading from the gospel of Luke, chapter 4, verses 5 through 8:

Reader 3: Then the devil took him up

Reader 1: and showed him

Reader 2: in a second

Reader 3: all the kingdoms of the world.

Reader 1: "I will give you

Reader 2: all this power

Reader 3: *power*

Reader 1: *power*

Reader 2: and all this *wealth*

Reader 3: all this wealth," the devil told him.

Reader 1: "It has all been handed over to me,

Reader 2: and I can give it to anyone I choose. All this will be yours, then, *if*

Reader 3: if you worship me."

Reader 2: Jesus answered,

Reader 1: "The scripture says:

All: 'Worship the Lord your God and serve only him.' "

Pastoral Reflection on the temptations of the world [man's way vs. God's way] including philosophies, systems, values, power struggles, and more. Suggested scripture references: Proverbs 1:1-7; 3:5-12; 1 Corinthians 1:17—3:23; Colossians 2:8—3:17; 1 John 2:15-17.

Personal Reflection And Silent Prayer

Reader 3: A reading from the gospel of Luke, chapter 4, verses 9 through 13:

Reader 1: Then the devil took him to the highest point in Jerusalem

Reader 2: and set him on the highest point of the temple

Reader 3: and said to him, "If you are God's Son, throw yourself down from here.

Reader 2: For the scripture says, 'God will order his angels to take good care of you.' It also says, 'They will hold you up with their hands so that not even your feet will be hurt on the stones.' "

Reader 1: But Jesus answered, "The scripture says, 'Do not

Reader 2: do *not*

Reader 3: do not put the Lord your God to the test.' "

Pastoral Reflection on the temptations of the devil [false gods vs. one, true God] including the occult, cults, humanism, and the like. Suggested scripture references: 1 Corinthians 10; 1 Thessalonians 5:19-20; John 8:31-59; 1 John 2:18-27; 4:1-6; 2 John 7-11.

Personal Reflection And Silent Prayer

Finding Victory In The Wilderness

All sing: "The cross before me, the world behind me (3x) / No turning back, no turning back"

Reader 4: During these next forty days, let us remember Jesus' experience in the wilderness — how he met the temptations of the devil with the Word of God, how he fasted and prayed, and how the angels ministered to him.

Reader 1: "If we are tempted by such trials, we must not say, "This temptation comes from God." For God cannot be tempted by evil, and he himself tempts no one. We are tempted when we are drawn away and trapped by our own evil desires." James, chapter 1, verses 13 and 14.

Reader 2: "This means that he (Jesus) had to become like his people in every way, in order to be their faithful and merciful high priest in his service to God, so that the people's sins would be forgiven. And now he can help those who are tempted, because he himself was tempted and suffered." Hebrews, chapter 2, verses 17 and 18.

Reader 3: "If you think you are standing firm, you had better be careful that you do not fall. Every test that you have experienced is the kind that normally comes to people. But God keeps his promise, and he will not allow you to be tested beyond your power to remain firm; at the same time you are put to the test, he will give you the strength to endure it, and so provide you with a way out." First Corinthians, chapter 10, verses 12 and 13.

Reader 5: "Then war broke out in heaven. Michael and his angels fought against the dragon, who fought back with his angels; but the dragon was defeated, and he and his angels were not allowed to stay in heaven any longer. The huge dragon was thrown out — that ancient serpent, named the devil, or Satan, that deceived the whole world. He was thrown down to earth, and all his angels with him. Then I heard a loud voice in heaven saying, 'Now God's salvation has come! Now God has shown his power as King! Now his Messiah has shown his authority! For the one who stood before our God and accused believers day and night has been thrown out of heaven. They won the victory over him by the blood of the Lamb, and by the truth which they proclaimed, and they were willing to give up their lives and die.' " Revelation, chapter 12, verses 7 through 11.

Reader 1: "So I am ashamed of all I have said and repent in dust and ashes." Job, chapter 42, verse 6.

Hymn: "I Need Thee Ev'ry Hour"

Imposition Of Ashes/Dismissal

Optional Music during the Imposition of Ashes: "Renueva Me, Senor Jesus," "Create In Me A Clean Heart," "Draw Me Nearer," "Am I A Soldier Of The Cross?" "How Firm A Foundation," "My Soul, Be On Thy Guard," "Rise Up, O Men Of God")

We Are But Ashes

*Ash Wednesday Introduction
And Worship Service*

William Luoma

We Are But Ashes

Introduction

It was Ash Wednesday, and a woman sitting in a crowded Catholic church leaned over to the young man next to her and asked, "What is it that brings so many people out on a cold night, to get a little dirt smeared on their foreheads, and to be reminded that they are sinners and that they are going to die?" He looked at her somewhat oddly and said, "It's habit, I guess."

It must be more than habit. Ash Wednesday strikes a responsive chord in many people. Its theme has a peculiar appeal. It is a time to reflect that we are sinners, that life is finite, and that we are but ashes. But, it is something we need to do on occasion. It is a time to confront the failings of ourselves and of our society. It is a time to lay it all on the table and to see who we are and what we are. The mood is penitence and reflection on the quality of our faith and life.

The Ashes

Although many Protestant churches observe Ash Wednesday, a lesser number have actually used the tradition of the imposition of ashes on the foreheads of worshipers. If this is a new practice for your congregation, it will certainly be wise to discuss it well in advance with the proper worship or planning committee; also, announce it in such a way that worshipers will know that the imposition of ashes will be entirely a voluntary matter. For those persons who wish to use this tradition, the use of ashes can be a very significant symbolic act to enhance the meaning of Ash Wednesday worship.

Ashes can either be purchased or prepared beforehand. In liturgical tradition, "Ashes are prepared for this service by burning palm (or olive) branches from the previous Palm Sunday and grinding the ashes into powder by working them through a wire mesh sieve with a spoon and perhaps mixing the ashes with a little water or oil."[1] Place the mixture in a small shallow vessel or a glass dish from which the ashes can be imposed. Provide a damp towel or napkin for cleansing the minister's hands after the imposition.

Ashes may be prepared privately or as part of the Shrove Tuesday activity in the congregation. As a conclusion of this "eve of the Fast" celebration, the palms could be burned in a fireplace or in the church in a clean, outdoor barbeque grill. Cut the palms into short pieces to facilitate burning. If branches from the previous Palm Sunday are not available, a local florist may have some at a nominal cost. Do not use ashes from someone's fireplace, since there may be impurities or irritating substances in them.

When people come forward to receive the ashes, they may kneel or stand. The ashes are applied with the thumb in the form of a small cross on the forehead. The minister may use the words, "Remember that you are dust, and to dust you shall return," in addressing each person. Silence is more appropriate for this time than any music. It may be suggested to the congregation to meditate on Psalm 90 during the receiving of the sign of the cross with the ashes.

Suggestions For Planning

It is suggested to have three people assigned as Readers, to take the parts indicated in the "Ash Wednesday Reflections." Readers may also be responsible for the Old and New Testament scriptures.

Important: a number of sample headline news stories are listed in the Readers' parts of the Ash Wednesday Reflections. To make this really contemporary, take newspapers (or check television news) from two to three days prior to the service, and substitute current news stories that people will recognize. This needs to be done to make this section as meaningful as possible.

In the Ash Wednesday Reflections, Readers 2 and 3 should convey the impression that they are reading their news items directly from the newspaper. The burning of the newspaper symbolizes "taking the wrongdoings out of God's sight." In order to do this with a minimum of worry and risk, find a charcoal burner about table height, and have it in place with a few hot coals in it at the beginning of the service. Give the Readers a single sheet of newspaper (approximately 14"x20" or smaller), enough to show what is happening. The Reader can tear the paper into a manageable size, wrinkle it a bit, and place it on the hot coals. When the burning of the newspaper is completed, have someone remove the charcoal burner or firepit and place it outside or in a safe place, so that you and the congregation won't have to worry about it.

If an offering is customary, it may be included at the time of one of the hymns, or an offering basket may be placed at the door.

The Ash Wednesday Reflections, using news stories, is based on an original service written by Pat Schnapp, and was used at St. Thomas More Parish, in Bowling Green, Ohio.

---

1. Phillip H. Pfatteicher and Carlos R. Messerli, *Manual on the Liturgy — Lutheran Book of Worship* (Minneapolis: Augsburg Publishing House, 1979), p. 307.

We Are But Ashes

Worship Service

Quiet Meditation (*No Prelude*)

Invocation (*Minister*)   Romans 1:7; 2 Corinthians 1:3 (RSV)
    Grace to you and peace from God, our Father, and the Lord Jesus Christ. Blessed be the God and Father of our Lord Jesus Christ, the Father of mercies and God of all comfort.

Psalm 51 (*Unison*)   Selected verses — 1-4, 9-12 (NIV)
Have mercy on me, O God, according to your unfailing love; according to your great compassion blot out my transgressions. Wash away all my iniquity and cleanse me from my sin. For I know my transgressions, and my sin is always before me. Against you, you only, have I sinned and done what is evil in your sight.

Hide your face from my sins and blot out all my iniquity. Create in me a pure heart, O God, and renew a steadfast spirit within me. Do not cast me from your presence or take your Holy Spirit from me. Restore to me the joy of your salvation and grant me a willing spirit to sustain me.

Prayer (*Minister*)   *People*
Almighty God, you love all your children, and do not hate them for their sins. Help us to face up to ourselves to admit we are in the wrong, and to reach with confidence for your mercy; in Jesus Christ the Lord. Amen. (From *The Worshipbook*, Westminster Press, 1970 Joint Committee on Worship for Presbyterian Churches, p. 142.)

Hymn   "Beneath The Cross Of Jesus"

Ash Wednesday Reflections
Reader 1: Sound the trumpet in Zion! Order a fast! Proclaim a solemn assembly! Call the people together, summon the community, assemble the elders, gather the children, even the infants at the breast. Let the bridegroom leave his bedroom and the bride her alcove. Between vestibule and altar let the priests, the ministers of the people, lament.

(As a symbolic gesture of penitence, the minister may approach the altar and kneel during a moment of silence.)

Minister: Spare your people, Lord! Do not make your heritage a thing of shame, a mockery to the nations! Why should outsiders say, "Where is their God?" Let us return to the Lord with all our heart, fasting, mourning, and weeping.

Reader 1: Cry out full-throated and unsparingly, lift up your voice like a trumpet blast! Tell my people their wickedness and the house of Jacob their sins. Do you call this a fast, a day acceptable to the Lord?

(The next few readings by Readers 2 and 3 should be replaced with current events.)

Reader 2: A seven-year-old girl, who got off the school bus three blocks from her home, disappeared and never made it home. Last week, her name was put on the missing child list.

Reader 3: In Common Pleas Court, an area man pleaded guilty yesterday to passing bad checks.

Reader 2: A Los Angeles woman was found guilty of four charges of trafficking in obscenity in Miami, Florida.

Reader 1: Do you call this a fast, a day acceptable to the Lord?

Reader 3: A Chicago financier has been accused of fraud by a grand jury and awaits sentencing.

Reader 2: Trial dates have been set for three persons charged in connection with the January death of a Detroit man found in his home with his throat cut. One of the persons charged is his son, aged nineteen.

Reader 3: A man, convicted of trying to extort two million dollars from an airline by planting a bomb, was sentenced Wednesday to twelve years in prison.

Reader 1: Do you call this a fast, a day acceptable to the Lord?

Reader 2: Crosses were burned and shots were fired outside of the homes of three black families in a northern city last night.

Reader 3: Police are questioning acquaintances of a twelve-year-old girl bludgeoned to death last week in an abandoned theater. She had been sexually molested.

Reader 2: A freshman student died at the University of Michigan during a hazing incident that one fraternity member described as "cruel and sick, but not unusual."

Reader 1: Do you call this a fast, a day acceptable to the Lord? Take your wrongdoings out of my sight.

(Readers 2 and 3 burn their newspapers.)

Reader 1: Rend your hearts and not your garments, and return to the way of the Lord.

Old Testament Reading for Ash Wednesday   Jonah 3:1-10

Minister or Reader: The name of Jonah is a familiar name. He was a reluctant prophet who ended up accomplishing God's purpose. These verses describe Jonah's warning and Nineveh's remarkable response to it. *(Read Jonah 3:1-10.)*

New Testament Reading   James 4:13-17

Minister or Reader: In the second lesson, James reminds us of the uncertainty and the shortness of human life. *(Read James 4:13-17.)*

The Gospel   Luke 18:9-14

Minister: One of the familiar parables of Jesus is this one in the gospel of Saint Luke, in which he compares the attitudes of two men who went to the temple to pray. *(Read Luke 18:9-14.)* This is the Word of the Lord.

Hymn   "Where Cross The Crowded Ways Of Life"
                                                   or "Dear Lord And Father Of Mankind"

A Message for Ash Wednesday

Receiving The Sign Of The Cross With Ashes *(Voluntary for those who desire)*
Minister: Ashes are a sign of repentance, humility, and frailty. They remind us of our total dependence on God. Before you approach to receive the sign of the cross with ashes, reflect on the meaning of this action:

Do you accept responsibility for your personal sins? (You may answer, "I do.")

Do you accept responsibility for that evil in the world that your apathy and indifference have allowed? (You may answer, "Yes.")

Do you desire to return to the Lord with your whole heart, and to seek his forgiveness and strength? (You may answer, "I do.")

Do you believe that, to be a follower of Jesus, you must deny yourself and take up your cross daily? (You may answer, "I believe.")

Do you believe it is foolish to work for great achievements or success if you destroy your soul in the process? (You may answer, "Yes.")

Do you believe in the mercy of God, which is constant and more vast than all the evil in the world? (You may answer, "Yes, I believe.")

Take now, then, these ashes, and return to the Lord with your whole heart.

(People may come forward, and either kneeling or standing, receive the sign of the cross with ashes on their foreheads. The minister may say these words to each person: "Remember that you are dust, and to dust you shall return.")

Reader 1: From bonfire and arsonist's blaze, from the coal stove and the crematorium — ashes blighted with mortality, we carry ourselves to the ash pile of our deaths, yet reminding: There is no lasting city here, to dust we shall return.

Reader 2: A gray smudge on our foreheads like our smudged, imperfect lives, streaked with self-ishness, singed by the angers, jealousies, greed, and lust that flame within, dying embers of good intentions compromised, forgotten. Ashen remains of resolutions soon burnt out.

Reader 3: As we wear the sign of the cross with ashes, we enter our Lent, to emerge, like the Phoenix, fresh-fashioned on Easter.

The Lord's Prayer (*Unison*)

The Benediction
May the warmth of his love, the light of his truth, and the peace of his promise go with you and remain with you. Amen.

Hymn
"I Lay My Sins On Jesus"
or "Take Up Your Cross, The Savior Said"

Your King Comes!

Palm Sunday Celebration

Janice Bennett Wyatt

Your King Comes!

Worship Service

(Note before we worship: Children and youth seated at the ends of the pews will distribute palms to you as you enter. Adults are requested to assist the children with following the service and guiding them if necessary. We are all part of the family of God; let us help one another! Think on these things: Is our church really acting like a family? A family of God? What can I do to live out my part to help our church family to be closer to God?)

Prelude

Call To Worship
Leader: God is here! Let us rejoice at his presence.
People: Let us break forth in shouts of praise and in songs of joy!
Leader: Listen, O God, to our songs and our prayers and respond to the hearts that reach out for you. Amen.

Processional Hymn   "All Glory Laud And Honor"

Call To Penitence
O God, our King and our Lord, like the crowds that surrounded the Christ on that first Palm Sunday, we often praise you with our lips only to reject you in our hearts. Take disloyalty and unfaithfulness out of our lives and hear us now as we pray together asking for your forgiveness ...

Confession Of Sin *(Unison)*
Lord Jesus, as we celebrate your triumphal entry into Jerusalem, help me to search within myself to discover where I stand in the crowd. Am I among those who would deny you because you want me to do things in a way that is different? Do I really want you to be my king when you lead me to give and serve rather than take? Forgive me when I do not make the necessary effort to follow your teachings. Amen.

Kyrie   "Lord, Have Mercy Upon Us"

Assurance Of Pardon
Now hear this: God loves you whether you are with those who welcome Jesus or among those who deny him. Be assured God is your loving Father.
Minister: O Lord, open our lips
People: And our mouths shall show forth thy praise.

Gloria Patri

Litany Of Greatness[1] *(Based on Matthew 23:1-12)*

Leader: Greatness is not:

People: Letting the happiness of life pass us by, nor forgetting the joy of serving the Lord.

Leader: Greatness is not:

People: Preaching without practicing, laying heavy burdens on people.

Leader: Greatness is not:

People: Doing things to be seen by the crowd, always picking seats of honor at the banquets.

Leader: Greatness is:

People: Being a servant of the great God, who made heaven and earth, and being responsible for the world he has entrusted to us.

Leader: Greatness is:

People: Following the way of Jesus Christ and through the Spirit making ourselves available to those in need.

Leader: Greatness is:

People: Belonging to the church and making our ministry real in private and public life.

Unison: Greatness is bringing the greatness to God to bear on the greatness of the world's needs. O God, help us to be your servants and the servant of others around our world through Jesus Christ, our Lord. Amen.

Choral Anthem

Palm Sunday Drama   "Your King Comes!"

Hymn   "Rejoice, Ye Pure In Heart"

Prayers *(Pastoral Prayer and Lord's Prayer)*

Prayer Response

Concerns Of The Church

The Offertory Sentence

Receiving Of Tithes And Offering

The Offertory Anthem

Presentation Of The Offering And Doxology

Prayer Of Dedication

Recessional Hymn   "All Hail The Power Of Jesus' Name"

Benediction

Leader:	Christ be with us.
People:	**Christ be within us.**
Leader:	Christ be beside us.
People:	**Christ to win us.**
Leader:	Christ to comfort.
People:	**And restore us.**
Leader:	Christ beneath us.
People:	**Christ above us.**
Leader:	Christ behind us.
People:	**Christ before us.**
Leader:	Amen.
People:	**Amen.**

Benediction Response

Silent Meditations And Chimes

Postlude

---

1. Litany titled "Greatness Is" by David James Randolph, *Ventures in Worship* (Nashville, Tennessee: Abingdon Press, 1969), p. 60.

Your King Comes!

Palm Sunday Drama

Production Notes

This dramatic celebration of the triumphal entry of Jesus into Jerusalem is a "we-were-there" type of reenactment designed to give all the feeling and experience of being a part of the crowd on that day. It relies on the speaking voice and a minimum amount of action to create the feeling of participation. It is designed to be the sermon portion of your Palm Sunday morning worship service, the day some say is the Children's Day of Holy Week, as a procession or parade is something they can understand. It calls for the participation of children, youth, and adults and could be adapted for use in churches of many different sizes. Costumes and action could be added to make it more dramatic, however this also calls for more preparation time.

As printed here, the production could be presented without requiring extra rehearsal time outside of that already planned for church and church school. The first step would be a meeting of the teachers for a full reading of the script. They then could choose children and youth to which the parts would be assigned. Teachers could enlist the participation of those in their own classes, hand out marked scripts, and ask those chosen to memorize the part underlined as well as to read and become familiar with the entire script. A reading of the script and assignment of locations could take place during the church school time on one of the Sundays prior to Palm Sunday. On Palm Sunday itself the final rehearsal could take place during the church school time if it precedes your regular morning worship service.

It is suggested that the children and youth participating be seated at the ends of the pews, both on the main aisle and at the far ends of the rows. They should be in their places about thirty minutes prior to the beginning of the service and each should have a small bundle of palms. As the congregation is seated, the participants would hand a palm to all who come to sit in their rows. Nursery, kindergarten, and first grade members might come in closer to the beginning of the service and sit in groups near the front.

Key to the entire production would be planning and rehearsing enough so that the voices can be heard by all. Remind participants that the parts need to be spoken clearly and with a loud voice, such as one would use when calling a message to someone upstairs or way down on a lower level. If the various parts are memorized, the production will be more effective. All participants and teachers need a copy of the script to clue them as to when their parts come.

You might choose to use the service suggested here beginning on page 25 or design your own. The service bulletin should relay the fact that the congregation is asked by the narrator to join in the reenactment by repeating the words of praise as indicated and by standing and raising their palms when requested.

The narrator should be a strong leader — either the pastor or another leader with a well-trained voice and a compelling manner. The two interpreters would most likely be chosen from among your youth. These three should schedule a rehearsal in addition to those scheduled for all participants. The twelve disciples could wear large cardboard name tags so all could easily read their names. This would make the experience even more educational. In addition to the above, there are about thirty voices, some more childlike than others. If your presenting group is smaller in number, some could take two parts. In order to have even the smallest children's voices heard, you will find that nursery, kindergarten, and first-grade children are best treated as groups. Each group has a sentence that should be spoken in unison. These lines could be practiced several times in their own classrooms.

Participants stand when it is time for their parts and remain standing until the end of the hymn that follows the reenactment. Suggested locations in the sanctuary for participants: Seat the twelve disciples on the main aisle and have them face the center when they stand. Those who speak first should be seated toward the rear and those who speak later should be seated in the middle and front pews. This will give the illusion that the procession is moving forward. The couple owning the colt should be near the back and those speaking after that should be placed in the middle and front pews. Those participants who seem to be in conversation with one another should be placed near each other. The Jesus voice should be a strong one with the ability to convey calmness and conviction. This voice should come from the balcony or another strategic location where the person would not be in full view.

Characters

Narrator	Family	Simon
Interpreter 1 and 2	Child 1 and 2	Scribe 1 and 2
Jesus	Mother and Father	John
Bartholomew	Villagers 1-16	Thomas
Owner of Colt	Pharisee 1 and 2	Thaddaeus
Andrew	Mary	Simon Peter
Owner's Wife	Martha	Kindergarten
Matthew	Child 3 and 4	Nursery
Philip	James 1 and 2	First Grade
		Loud Adult

(Adults are asked by the Narrator to join in the reenactment by repeating words of praise as indicated and by standing and raising their palms.)

Narrator: Jesus was with his disciples traveling toward Jerusalem, as it was the time of the Passover.

Interpreter 1: Jewish people came to Jerusalem from all over the Mediterranean world so that they could celebrate the Feast of the Passover in the holy city. The most important temple, the center of all Judaism, was within the city walls.

Interpreter 2: The Passover celebration helped them to remember that God had led their forebears out of slavery in Egypt to a land of their own. God had watched over them and protected them as they traveled. He had made it possible for them to be free persons, no longer bound to serve a master whose aims were not their aims.

Narrator: They traveled to Jerusalem in caravans. Many came on foot, walking every step of the way; others traveled by riding on a donkey or a camel; some even came by ship.

Interpreter 1: Before Passover was to be celebrated, the Jews mended all the roads and bridges, painted the family tombs, and washed all the household utensils. Each family threw away all the old leaven that was left from their bread-making. They did this to remember the time their forefathers had to leave Egypt quickly without any provisions for their journey.

Interpreter 2: Jews came from throughout the countryside to Jerusalem to purify themselves once more and to partake of the feast with their families.

Narrator: And so it was that Jesus and the disciples traveled together toward Jerusalem, as was the custom. They went even though Jesus knew it might be dangerous for him.

Interpreter 1: The journey was a slow one. Jesus and the disciples stopped along the way to teach, to heal, to see friends, and to greet strangers who had questions.

Interpreter 2: See, now they are approaching the city gate; let's pretend we are there. We can hear Jesus say ...

Jesus: Andrew, Bartholomew, go into the village over there outside the wall, and just as you are entering, you will see a colt hitched to a post. It's a colt on which no one has ever ridden. Loosen him and bring him here.

Bartholomew: But Master, what shall we say to the owners if they ask why we are untethering him?

Jesus: Simply say, the Lord has need of him and they will understand and let you bring him to me. We will return it later.

Narrator: This was done, John explains in his gospel, because it was written in the scriptures studied at that time. We now call that book Zechariah in the Old Testament. You will find the verse in Zechariah, chapter 9, verses 9-11.

Interpreter 1: Rejoice greatly, O daughter Zion! Shout aloud, O daughter Jerusalem! Lo, your king comes to you; triumphant and victorious is he, humble and riding on a donkey, on a colt, the foal of a donkey. He will cut off the chariot Ephraim and the war horse from Jerusalem; and the battle bow shall be cut off, and he shall command peace to the nations; his dominion shall be from sea to sea, and from the river to the ends of the earth.

Narrator: And they that were sent, went their way and came to the place where the colt was tied, and everything was exactly as Jesus had told them. They began to unloosen the tether ...

Interpreter 2: The owners of the colt were nearby and called out ...

Owner of Colt: Stop! Why are you unloosening my colt?

Andrew: Jesus of Nazareth sent us to get him. He said to tell you the Lord has need of him.

Owner of Colt: Jesus of Nazareth? If that is so, take the colt to Jesus. I have heard of the great things he is doing in the name of the Lord. I am glad to help him. Where is Jesus? I would like to meet him.

Bartholomew: Come along. Many seem to be gathering along the roads who also want to catch a glimpse of him.

Andrew: Yes, they have heard that he raised Lazarus from death to life.

Owner's Wife: Look! A great crowd is gathering. Hurry, I want to be a part of it.

Narrator: The chief priest and Pharisees seem to be gathering over there — they don't seem in the mood to celebrate.

Interpreter 1: No, the chief priests, scribes, and Pharisees, the leaders of the Jewish religion, the keepers of the law, were against Jesus as his teachings were different from theirs; they could not believe he was truly the Son of God.

Andrew: Here's the colt, Jesus. Come sit upon his back so all can see you above the crowd.

Matthew: I'll put my robe on him for you to sit on.

Philip: Here's mine, too. The crowds are getting larger. Be careful, Jesus. We must stay together.

Child 1: Give me that palm branch, Father, so I might wave it.

Mother: I have picked these flowers. I'll throw them in front of him so he knows we like what he is doing and saying.

Child 2: I want to see the new king. Will he save us from the Romans?

Father: I wonder. He tells us to love everyone, but how can we love those who plot against us?

Villager 1: There is much of his teaching that seems hard to follow, but wouldn't we have a wonderful world if all could love their neighbors as they love their own families? But it is so hard to do.

Villager 2: There he comes; I see him. Welcome to the Son of the family of David!

Family and Villagers 1 and 2: Hosanna! Blessed be he who comes in the name of the Lord!

Pharisee 1: You see, the world has gone after him, the only way to stop him is to arrest him.

Pharisee 2: We must move quickly now. I wonder if we could persuade one of his followers to help us?

Villager 3: I'm going to throw my robe out for him to go over; that will show him and everyone that he is important.

Villager 4: I'll cover this part of the way with branches from the palm tree.

Family: Hosanna to the Son of David!

Villagers 1-4: Hosanna in the highest — Hosanna! Blessed be he who comes in the name of the Lord.

Villager 5: He healed the blind man you know.

Villager 6: He helped me to walk again. I had been crippled for so long.

Mary: It is so wonderful that he was able to raise our brother Lazarus from the death that had overtaken him.

Martha: I still can hardly believe it is true. God is truly with Jesus.

Villager 7: Rejoice! Rejoice! Here comes the prophet Jesus.

Villager 8: He is from Nazareth of Galilee, you know. I know the family.

Villager 9: He cured my daughter who was ill for such a long time; we thought she would never be well again.

Child 3: I like the way he tells us stories. He even plays games with us. It is good to be near him.

James 1: Isn't it great to be welcomed to Jerusalem like this? Jesus' teachings have been heard by many — our world will be a better place because of his teachings.

Simon: Yes, I believe he is God's Son. Otherwise, how could he perform such miracles and speak with real authority? Hundreds want to hear him talk and teach.

Villager 10: I hear he cured a man of leprosy.

Philip: You're right. I was there when he did it ... and he is not the only one that Jesus has healed. It seems he can heal anyone who really believes he can do it. Jesus is truly close to God.

Scribe 1: Watch carefully now. Stay close so we might hear what the man teaches. He will surely disobey one of the laws, just as when he picked the wheat on the sabbath day.

Scribe 2: Don't worry, I'll watch. I know we have to get him. I'll stay as close to him as I can. He is dangerous for these people — they think he really is their Savior. He will get us into trouble with the Romans.

Child 4: He's coming close to us now, Mother. I want to say hello to him. Lift me up so I can see him. I'll wave this palm branch so he sees me.

Villager 10: Blessed be he who comes in the name of the Lord.

Narrator: Let's call it out so he looks our way. Everyone now. Blessed is he who comes in the name of the Lord!

All: Blessed is he who comes in the name of the Lord.

John: Be careful, Master, the crowd is pressing closer to us. There are so many people. I'm glad they recognize you as their leader.

Thomas: But there are some in the crowd who are enemies, don't forget that. We will stay and watch on this side; you three watch along that side.

James 2: Is everyone here? Where is Judas? He is not with us now. I can't see him.

Thaddaeus: He stopped to talk to someone quite a ways back, he'll catch up.

Simon Peter: I'll go ahead — I'm tall enough to see above the crowd. I see the temple ahead now. Shall we head toward it, Master?

Villager 11: You know, about a year ago, Jesus looked at me and knew my thoughts. I've had a new life since then. He is truly amazing, he is close to God.

Villager 12: He cured my sickness. I was out of my mind until I met him and he looked at me and healed me. Just like that — *(snaps fingers)*.

Villager 13: Let's just stand back here and watch. I don't want to participate. Someone might see us and think we are his followers.

Villager 14: Yes, I believe Jesus is a great leader, but I don't want to get involved. It is too dangerous.

Villager 15: That Jesus doesn't care who he talks to. He is seen with those who do wrong — sinners and even tax collectors.

Villager 16: I wonder what he wants from us. I wonder why he cares what we do.

Kindergarten: Hooray for Jesus!

Nursery: He loves everyone.

First Grade: Let's clap our hands and shout hooray!

Narrator: Let's all do as the children say — join in the clapping and shout hooray. *(begins clapping)*

All: Hooray!

Narrator: Hooray for Jesus!

All: Hooray for Jesus!

Narrator: Hosanna to the Son of David!

All: Hosanna to the Son of David!

Loud Adult: Be our king, Jesus. Save us from our oppressors, from those who treat us like servants, and make us pay high taxes.

Jesus: Listen to me — I want to be king of your heart and your mind. I want to lead you to love God with all your heart, and all your strength, and all your mind. I want to teach you to love your neighbor as yourself.

Narrator: Hosanna! Hosanna! Come, let us all stand, raise your palms high and shout Hosanna!

All: Hosanna!

Narrator: Blessed is he who comes in the name of the Lord.

All: Blessed is he who comes in the name of the Lord!

Narrator: Blessed is he who comes from on high!

All: Blessed is he who comes from on high!

Narrator: Hosanna in the highest!

All: Hosanna in the highest!

Narrator: Rejoice, you pure in heart — come — let's all sing it together.

Crown Him Lord Of All!

Sunday Of The Passion/Palm Sunday
Combination Worship Service

William Luoma

Crown Him Lord Of All!

Introduction

According to the three-year ecumenical lectionary, the Sunday before Easter is primarily known as the Sunday of the Passion, instead of Palm Sunday. The procession with palm branches is still recommended, but the emphasis of the day has shifted to the Passion of Christ, as seen in the suggested lengthy gospel readings appointed.

In this worship service, however, we have chosen to lift up the Palm Sunday theme, and to focus on the kingship of Christ and his triumphal entry into Jerusalem. Christ the king is a powerful image. Let the church become Jerusalem for this Sunday morning!

The use and distribution of palms is a unique custom. When else, and where else, do we ever use palms or hand them out? Palms are a memorable and meaningful symbol to many Christians. I think of Mike, a retired Army man living in southeastern Ohio. He can take a palm leaf, and weave it into an intricate, curled "designer cross," in a way he learned as a child. I think of Ray, a maintenance man in Illinois, who keeps some palm leaves in his car, "to ward off anything bad." I think of Ethel, in whose Bible there is a small cross made of palm leaves, pressed flat as a bookmark. I think of Catholic friends, who always seem to have a dried palm leaf sticking out from behind some picture on the wall, all year long.

Suggestions For Planning

Prior to the worship service, invite all children present to take part in a procession with palms. Gather the children into a nearby room where palms can be distributed. During the processional hymn, have the minister or another leader lead the children in a procession through the aisles of the sanctuary. A crucifer and a banner carrier may also be included in the procession. Ask the children to hold their palms high. Dismiss them at the end of the processional hymn to go to their seats.

For the children's message, "The Two Crowns," some visual aid should be used. The two crowns may be prepared beforehand as drawings, or simple models may be made from paper. Some churches may have a kingly crown in their box of Christmas costumes for wise men. An actual crown of thorns is a very effective object lesson.

The hymn, "Crown Him With Many Crowns," serves as a focal point in the worship service. A spoken introduction is provided for each of the three stanzas used. As a lay reader reads each introduction, ask the organist to play through the stanza softly, as background music. The reader and the organist can easily pace themselves, with a minimum of rehearsal time, to have the reading and the music completed at the same time.

Stanzas for the hymn, "Crown Him With Many Crowns," vary from hymnal to hymnal. If the congregation is to sing the stanzas from the church hymnal, check the number and the order of the stanzas ahead of time.

Crown Him Lord Of All!

Worship Service

Processional Hymn   "Onward, Christian Soldiers" or "Lead On, O King Eternal"

Invocation

Minister: Blessed is he who comes in the name of the Lord!
People: Hosanna in the highest!
Minister: Blessed is he who comes in the name of the Lord!
People: Hosanna to the Son of David!
Minister: In the name of the Father, and of the Son, and of the Holy Spirit. Amen.

Psalm 24

Men: **The earth is the Lord's and the fullness thereof,**
Women: **The world and those who dwell therein;**
Men: **For he has founded it upon the seas,**
Women: **And established it upon the rivers.**
Men: **Who shall ascend the hill of the Lord?**
Women: **And who shall stand in his holy place?**
Men: **He who has clean hands and a pure heart,**
Women: **Who does not lift up his soul to what is false, and does not swear deceitfully.**
Men: **He will receive blessing from the Lord,**
Women: **And vindication from the God of his salvation.**
Men: **Such is the generation of those who seek him,**
Women: **Who seek the face of the God of Jacob.**
Men: **Lift up your heads, O gates! And be lifted up, O ancient doors!**
Women: **That the King of glory may come in.**
Men: **Who is the King of glory?**
Women: **The Lord, strong and mighty, the Lord, mighty in battle!**
Men: **Lift up your heads, O gates! And be lifted up, O ancient doors!**
Women: **That the King of glory may come in.**
Men: **Who is this King of glory?**
Women: **The Lord of hosts, he is the King of glory!**

Prayer

Lord God, our heavenly Father: you have called us to be citizens of your kingdom on earth. You have called us to trust and love you with our hearts and our souls, our minds and our strength. Today as we recall the welcome your Son received as a king in Jerusalem, and the opposition to him several days later; we pray that we will not be the kind of followers who praise him one day and forsake him the next. Keep us faithful to our calling as his disciples. In Jesus' name. Amen.

Hymn   "O Worship The King" or "The Son Of God Goes Forth To War"

First Lesson   Zechariah 9:9-10

In these verses, the prophet Zechariah looks ahead and describes his vision of the coming one of God.

Second Lesson   1 Timothy 1:12-17

Paul writes to Timothy, comparing his former life with his Christian faith. He sees Christ as a glorious king.

Gospel   Luke 19:28-40

Luke tells of the arrangements that were made for Jesus to enter Jerusalem, and describes the response of the crowd.

Children's Message   "The Two Crowns"

Good morning, boys and girls, and thank you for taking part in the Palm Sunday procession today. On this one Sunday of the year, we use palm branches to remind us of something special about Jesus. Jesus was in a parade. People shouted and welcomed him. They even laid their garments in the road to make a path for him. They greeted him as a king.

Here is a crown, one that could be worn by a king. Tell me, how do you get to be a king? Would you be elected like we elect our president? Or, would you have to be born into a royal family?

The answer is that you usually have to be born into a royal family. Remember when Jesus was born, and the wise men came? They were looking for a king. They knew he was a special person. We know he is the Son of God.

A king has certain duties. He is supposed to lead his country. He is there to protect and watch over his people. Jesus is a king, but he doesn't have an earthly kingdom. He is a different kind of king. He is a king of our hearts.

Now, look at this crown. Yes, this is a crown. It's made of sharp thorns. If you took this in your hands, you'd get scratched and have thorns in your skin. This is a cruel crown. It is one that no one should ever wear on his head. But it is the kind of crown that Jesus had to wear. His enemies put it on his head and it hurt. It was part of the suffering Jesus went through for us. This crown is a symbol of hate and unkindness.

Jesus is our king. But, he does not need to wear either crown any more. His kingdom is here within us. He is the king of our hearts and lives. He wants what is best for us for us, and we can trust him. He watches over us and we love him because he cares for us.

You have a king and I have a king. His name is Jesus. We call him Lord. I hope you will be his always.

Hymn   "Crown Him With Many Crowns"

Reader: *(reads while one stanza of the hymn is played softly)* The hymn we are about to sing, "Crown Him With Many Crowns," is one that reflects the mood of that first Palm Sunday when Jesus entered Jerusalem. The crowds greeted him with shouts of "Hosanna!" They called him the Son of David.

We greet him as our king, not only for a day, but for all time. He is the Lamb of God, and there is none like him, for he is a matchless king through all eternity. Let us sing stanza _____ *(check your hymnal for number)*.

All: Crown him with many crowns,
The Lamb upon his throne;
Hark! how the heav'nly anthem drowns
All music but its own!
Awake my soul, and sing
Of him who died for three,
And hail him as thy matchless king
Through all eternity.

Reader: *(reads while music plays softly)* Matthew Bridges and Godfrey Thring have given us a great hymn that describes the Lord of love! That love is evident in the wounds in his hands and his side. He suffered for us; he died for us. Greater love has no man than this, that a man lay down his life for his friends.

    Jesus said, "This is my commandment, that you love one another as I have loved you." In him we see how God so loved the world that he gave his only Son. Let us sing stanza _____.

All: Crown him the Lord of love —
Behold his hands and side,
Rich wounds, yet visible above,
In beauty glorified.
No angels in the sky
Can fully bear that sight,
But downward bend their burning eyes
At mysteries so bright.

Reader: *(reads while music plays softly)* We sing of Christ, the Lord of life, who triumphed o'er the grave! Each time we gather, we proclaim his victory over death. He said, "I am the resurrection and the life, he who believes in me, though he were dead, yet shall he live!" No one else can offer us eternal life. He came that we might have life, and have it more abundantly. He said, "Be faithful unto death, and I will give you the crown of life." Let us sing stanza _____.

All: Crown him the Lord of life,
Who triumphed o'er the grave
And rose victorious in the strife
For those he came to save.
His glories now we sing,
Who died and rose on high,
Who died, eternal life to bring,
And lives that death may die.

Sermon   "The Credentials Of A King"

Apostles' Creed

Offering

General Prayer

Dear heavenly Father: We have come together to worship you. We feel the warmth of your love and mercy, and the inner strength and peace you give us through your Holy Spirit.

You know this congregation; and you know each one of us well. You have called us to your kingdom's work, and you know how hesitant we often are. You know how many excuses we dream up, and how many other things come first in our lives.

Remind us again of the urgency of what we are about. Let this congregation be a real light in the community, and let our love for one another be genuine.

Forgive us for calling ourselves Christians when we are only poor imitations. Have mercy on us when we let other things crowd out the example of your Son, Jesus Christ.

We pray about the problems facing our world. Bless those who are trying to help the homeless, so that people do not have to suffer. For those places where there is famine and lack of food, stir up those of us who can do something about it, so the hungry may find food, just as the Israelites found manna many years ago.

Give to our president and all governing officials good health and protection that they may guide this country wisely and faithfully. Give innovative thinking and patience to those who meet on behalf of the nations, to seek and work for peace.

Here, in this parish, we need your Spirit. Use our efforts to reach out, so that people who are still outside the kingdom, may enter and find joy. Take our feeble attempts to show love, and change them, as your Son did when he changed the water to wine, so that the true gospel may be seen by those who say they have no use for it.

In places where people are needed to serve, raise them up to respond to your call. Enable this congregation to be a growing family of believers so that we can do more witnessing for Christ instead of worrying about finances.

Touch each home and each individual here with your love and peace. To those who are suffering, give relief. To those who are anxious, give peace. To those who are discouraged, give hope. To those bearing a load of guilt, give the assurance of forgiveness.

Give us a sense of unity as people of your kingdom. Let there be nothing to divide us or to take away from our mission for Christ. We pray in the words he has taught us ...

The Lord's Prayer

Benediction

Hymn   "Ride On, Ride On In Majesty"

41

Crown Him Lord Of All!

Sermon

The Credentials Of A King

And Pilate asked him, "Are you the King of the Jews?" And he answered him, "You have said so."
— Luke 23:3

Many of you have experienced the hassle of trying to cash a check in a place where you are not known. No matter how honest you try to look, all you may get is a polite, "I'm sorry, we don't accept checks."

That is undoubtedly the reason for the popularity of credit, check, and charge cards. A credit card can easily get you a room, a meal, fill up your tank, or will be accepted for some of those impulse purchases. With nothing more than a small piece of plastic, and our signatures, strangers will allow us to charge a variety of expenses. In that sense, the cards that we carry serve as our credentials.

Think for a moment of a king. Today is the day we traditionally acknowledge Jesus as king. What kind of credentials would a person have to carry to prove that he was indeed a king? If he wore a crown, would that be enough? If he carried a scepter and had on a long, purple robe, would that suffice?

When Jesus entered Jerusalem, he carried no credentials but himself, yet he was welcomed as a king. What is there about Jesus that helps me to know he is a king? What are his credentials?

His credentials certainly are not seen in documents, driver's licenses, letters, or credit cards. His credentials are more readily seen in his demeanor before his enemies.

Someone else in his position might have made a desperate appeal for freedom, or might have been willing to recant, or lie his way out of it.

Someone else who could perform miracles might have worked some wonder for Herod in order to gain a recommendation for release.

Someone else in Jesus' shoes might have tried to bargain with Pilate, or with his accusers.

Not Jesus. Here is a true king.

1. *This is a king who commands respect.* As Jesus stood before those who accused him, he appeared as one who commanded respect. When Pilate asked, "Do you not hear how many things they testify against you?" Jesus gave no answer, not even to a single charge. Pilate "wondered greatly" (Matthew 27:13-14). Jesus had "set his face" (like flint, according to Isaiah 50:7), to go to Jerusalem, a city where he knew hostility awaited him. He knew the kind of welcome he would receive. "Behold, we are going up to Jerusalem; and the Son of Man will be delivered to the chief priests and scribes, and they will condemn him to death, and deliver him to the Gentiles to be mocked and scourged and crucified, and he will be raised on the third day" (Matthew 20:17-19).

It is because of this that Jesus commands respect. In spite of the evil treatment he received, he showed himself a king. We marvel at his courage. He didn't have to do it. He could have called down twelve legions of angels and dazzled his enemies with his power, but he didn't (Matthew 26:53). He fulfilled his mission. He became obedient unto death, even death on a cross.

In Mark Twain's *The Adventures of Tom Sawyer*, there is an incident in which Tom and Becky Thatcher are both in the schoolroom under the stern schoolmaster, Mr. Dobbins. While the teacher was out of the room, Becky accidentally tore a page in one of his personal books. When Mr. Dobbins discovered the damaged page, he was furious. His menacing gaze searched every face for some sign of guilt. He began interrogating each one by name.

"Benjamin Rogers, did you tear this book?" A denial.

"Joseph Harper, did you?" Another denial.

"Amy Lawrence?" A shake of the head.

"Gracie Miller?" The same sign.

The next girl was Becky Thatcher. Her face was white with terror. At that instant, Tom Sawyer, knowing that she would buckle under the pressure, impulsively sprang to his feet and shouted, "I done it!"

The schoolmaster turned angrily on Tom, gave him the whipping, and made him stay after school for two hours.

Becky, who waited for him outside, was filled with gratitude, and said, "Tom, how could you be so noble?"

He didn't have to do it, but he did.

When we say that of Jesus, we are saying that he is a king who commands respect.

2. *This is a king who deserves loyalty.* If a king does not have loyal subjects, he is in trouble. The book of Proverbs says, "What is desired in a man is loyalty" (Proverbs 19:22). A loyal person is not a fair-weather friend. The loyal person is one who is there, not only in the good times, but also in times of trouble, disappointment, crisis, or grief.

It seems right, under normal circumstances, that a king ought to expect loyalty from his subjects. But it is also necessary for the king to be the kind of person who is worthy and deserving of their loyalty.

There is a story from long ago, of a king of a small province in Europe. This king had an exaggerated idea of his importance, and called a feast to celebrate his birthday. He invited his noblemen, stating that each one should bring a flask of his best wine to the celebration in honor of the king. The wine would be poured into one barrel to make the most exquisite beverage ever tasted in the kingdom.

One nobleman had little use for the king. So he took an empty flask, filled it with water, figuring that with all that wine, no one would ever know the difference.

At the feast, a large cask was placed at the banquet hall entrance. Each guest entered and poured a contribution into it. The nobleman who brought the water did likewise.

The great moment finally came. The king went over to the cask. He held out his goblet, ready for the best wine in the land. He opened the spigot and into his cup flowed pure water!

I wonder what comes out of the tap when God checks our loyalty, both as individuals and as a church. Jesus' followers had their loyalty put to the test on the night when he was betrayed. You and I have our loyalty tested day after day in what we do and what we say and what we are. Are we giving Christ the best wine?

3. *This is a king who inspires faith.* In order to exist in the world, you and I have to have faith in other people. For example, I have faith in the mechanic who installs new brakes on my car. You trust the pharmacist who makes up a prescription for your toddler. Most of us think nothing of stopping at a restaurant and eating a meal prepared by a cook whom we've never met.

Some people seem to easily inspire faith while others cause us to doubt them. There are some people we believe in, for whom we would do almost anything; but there are others for whom we don't wish to lift a finger. We find ourselves feeling cynical and skeptical of them.

While battling the Philistines, King David was camped at a place called the Cave of Adullam. He was tired of fighting and was longing for a taste of home. David said, wishing out loud, "O that someone would give me water to drink from the well of Bethlehem which is by the gate!"

Three of his most noble and faithful soldiers overheard the king, and took it upon themselves to go and get water from that well for him. It meant risking their necks, for they had to break through the camp of the Philistines to do it.

When they brought the water to David, however, he refused to drink it. He recognized how dangerous it had been to get the water, and he realized that this act showed how highly they regarded him. Instead of drinking it, he poured it out on the ground as an offering to the Lord. David had already shown his faith in his men, and these three were responding with faith and love for their king (1 Chronicles 11:15-19).

What about Christ? He, too, is a man who inspires faith. We don't have to question whether he's in it for the money; we don't have to wonder whether he's running for office; we don't have to doubt whether or not he really cares about us. Jesus challenges us who are often of little faith, "Believe in God, believe also in me."

4. *This is a king who offers hope.* In a tract that came across my desk some time ago, there was in bold print, a provocative question, intended to make the reader stop and think. The question was: "If you were to die tonight and stand before God and he were to ask you, 'Why should I let you into my heaven?' what would your answer be?"

Why should God let me in? What is there that I could take out to show him to prove that I was worthy to enter? What kind of credentials would I need?

Would it help to tell God that I was voted "the most likely to succeed" in my graduating class? Or that I went to church every Sunday for 29 years in one stretch without missing? Would it convince God if I told him that I never killed anyone, never stole anything important, never was unfaithful in marriage, and only lied a few times that I can remember? Would it help to tell him that I always put my dollar in the offering? Or that I sat for five hours one night with a sick friend?

Would it make a difference to God if I told him that I've suffered and worried quite a bit more than the average person has? Would any of these be enough?

I doubt it.

When I stand before the throne of God, there is not much that I will be able to pull out to show God what a good person I have been. What I consider to be the greatest deeds will probably look pretty small. God sees the heart. He knows that my motives are not always the highest nor are they the purest.

There is only one thing that will be worth anything on that day and that is our hope in the Savior, Christ the Lord. If my hope is built on Jesus' blood and righteousness, that will be enough. He alone can save us.

Jesus is a king who offers hope. He offers hope for a life in his kingdom where there will be no more crying, no more pain or suffering, and no more death. He offers us the hope of life eternal.

Jesus Christ has all the credentials of a king. Pilate's question, "Are you the king of the Jews?" was accurate, but didn't quite go far enough. Jesus is not only king of the Jews, but he is the king of all believers, of all generations, for all time.

What is there about Jesus that helps me to know that he is a king? What are his credentials?

1. He is a king who commands respect.
2. He is a king who deserves loyalty.
3. He is a king who inspires faith.
4. He is a king who offers hope.

He is my king. I hope he is yours as well.

Like A Rose

*A Contemplative Service
For Maundy Thursday*

Lynne Cragg

Like A Rose

Worship Service

Prelude "Were You There?"

Silent Meditation

The Coins

Reader 1 Luke 22:7-12

The Disciples Enter

Reader 2 Luke 22:13

Communion

Reader 3 Luke 22:14-20

Silent Meditation

Reader 4 Luke 22:21-22

The Dispute

Jesus Luke 22:31-32

Peter Luke 22:33

Jesus Luke 22:34

Jesus And Disciples Leave

Song "Above All"

The Choice

Silent Meditation

Judas *(nonspeaking)*

Prayer Of Confession (*Unison*)

Christ my Savior, your death I chose to trust, yet I am found untrue. Your cross I agreed to bear, but the weight of my misery overcomes me. Your agony I yearn to embrace, but my own pain crushes my spirit. Your love I promised to share, yet my own interests claim priority.

Draw me closer, that I might be faithful; that my burden may strengthen me, that this pain might refine my spirit, and that your love may shine ever brighter. Amen.

Departure (*In silence*)

Like A Rose

Worship Service In Full Detail

Setting The Mood

The sanctuary is darkened with a light shining on the communion table, if possible. The table should be set up for communion with two added items: a single rose lying on the table and a pouch filled with coins. Both need to be visible to the congregation. Their inclusion will serve to arouse curiosity, but will not be clarified until the end of the service.

The readings can be shared by several people or narrated by one person. Either way, they occur from a selected spot under the lights.

The outline of the service is dedicated by the narrative reading of Luke 22.

Prelude

"Were You There?" is sung a cappella, the song is performed in a darkened corner, better if coming from the back of the sanctuary to put the focus on the words. This use of the song will make a stronger impact and will prepare the congregation for the message of the service. Include only the verses regarding Jesus' death.

Silent Meditation

After the solo, allow fifteen seconds of silence.

The Coins

The sound of thirty individual coins will then be heard being dropped on a hard surface, slowly, one by one. Again, this is heard, not seen. This is prerecorded or happens in a darkened corner with a microphone. Allow several seconds after the drop of the final coin before the reading.

Reader 1: Then came the day of Unleavened Bread, on which the Passover lamb had to be sacrificed. So Jesus sent Peter and John, saying, "Go and prepare the Passover meal for us that we may eat it." They asked him, "Where do you want us to make preparations for it?" "Listen," he said to them, "when you have entered the city, a man carrying a jar of water will meet you; follow him into the house he enters and say to the owner of the house, 'The teacher asks you, "Where is the guest room, where I may eat the Passover with my disciples?" ' He will show you a large room upstairs, already furnished. Make preparations for us there."

The Disciples Enter

The disciples can be dressed in everyday attire of today or in costume. Costumed disciples will be more readily identified, but disciples dressed in the style of today will help to make the connection between the choices they made that night and our own choices today.

They should sit in the first few rows, slightly staggered within the congregation, but together in small clusters, so they can talk with one another later.

Reader 2: *(begins reading when the disciples sit down)* So they went and found everything as he had told them; and they prepared the Passover meal.

Communion

It would be best if communion is served from the front as people come forward rather than serving the congregants in their pews. This way they can see the rose and bag of coins, but either tradition will work. The serving of communion is to take place while the third reader narrates verses 14-20.

Reader 3: *(reads while communion is being served)* When the hour came, he took his place at the table, and the apostles with him. He said to them, "I have eagerly desired to eat this Passover with you before I suffer; for I tell you, I will not eat it until it is fulfilled in the kingdom of God." *(pauses)* Then he took a cup, and after giving thanks he said, "Take this and divide it among yourselves; for I tell you that from now on I will not drink of the fruit of the vine until the kingdom of God comes." *(pauses)* Then he took a loaf of bread, and when he had given thanks he broke it and gave it to them, saying, "This is my body, which is given for you. Do this in remembrance of me." *(pauses)* And he did the same with the cup after supper, saying, "This cup that is poured out for you is the new covenant in my blood."

Silent Meditation

This lasts as long as the reader of the service deems effective. The silence of the meditation is broken by Jesus who quietly enters and stands at the front of the sanctuary, looking at his disciples.

Reader 4: But see, the one who betrays me is with me ... For the Son of Man is going as it has been determined, but woe to that one by whom he is betrayed!

The Dispute

At this point in the service, the disciples act out the question and denials that are referred to in verse 23. They address each other in their groups as well as looking to Jesus as they question his words. By being in the midst of the congregation, they are enabling the congregants to understand that we all have betrayed Jesus. Their improvised discussions begin with questions regarding who among them would betray Jesus, then move into denial of their own possible guilt. They may talk about which of them is unlikely to betray Jesus.

At this point, Jesus interrupts their discussions. He begins by addressing the disciples, but gradually includes the entire congregation gathered around them. This portion of the service should be memorized.

Jesus: The kings of the Gentiles lord it over them; and those in authority over them are called benefactors. But not so with you; rather the greatest among you must become like the youngest, and the leader like one who serves. For who is greater, the one who is at the table or the one who serves? Is it not the one at the table? But I am among you as one who serves.

You are those who have stood by me in my trials; and I confer on you, just as my Father has conferred on me, a kingdom, so that you may eat and drink at my table in my kingdom, and you will sit on thrones judging the twelve tribes of Israel. *(pauses, then looks directly at Peter)* Simon, Simon, listen! Satan has demanded to sift all of you like wheat, but I have prayed for you that your own faith may not fail; and you, when once you have turned back, strengthen your brothers.

Peter: *(quickly stands)* Lord, I am ready to go with you to prison and to death!

Jesus: I tell you, Peter, the cock will not crow this day, until you have denied three times that you know me.

(The lights go down.)

Jesus And Disciples Leave
Jesus and the disciples leave as the song, "Above All" begins.

Song   "Above All"
"Above All," written by Michael W. Smith, is performed live or a recording plays over the sound system. In either case, the words, as sung, are displayed on a video screen, if one is available. It is very important that the congregation catch the words of the song. If there is no screen available, then the words can be printed in the program. The words to "Above All" can be found at www.lyricsdownload.com/michael-w-smith-above-all-lyrics.html.

The Choice
At this point, the connection between Judas and ourselves begins as we consider the betrayal of Jesus.

Silent Meditation
The song is followed by a short period of silence to give time for reflection on the words. Have all the words displayed on the screen during this meditation.

Judas *(nonspeaking part)*
Silently, Judas comes in from the back of the sanctuary, walks up to the communion table, and picks up the rose. Then, slowly, with his other hand, he picks up the bag of coins. He stands looking at each one in turn, as if trying to decide what he will do, then he lets go of the rose, allowing it to fall on the floor. He holds the bag of coins tighter, turns, steps on the rose, crushing it, and walks out. Judas has made his choice.

Prayer Of Confession *(Unison)*
Christ my Savior, your death I chose to trust, yet I am found untrue. Your cross I agreed to bear, but the weight of my misery overcomes me. Your agony I yearn to embrace, but my own pain crushes my spirit. Your love I promised to share, yet my own interests claim priority.

Draw me closer, that I might be faithful; that my burden may strengthen me, that this pain might refine my spirit, and that your love may shine ever brighter. Amen.

Departure
The congregants depart from the service in silence, where they find crushed roses strewn all over the floor of the vestibule. There are enough roses lying around to make it impossible to avoid stepping on them. This is the final point of the service where the congregants connect their own betrayal of Jesus with that of Judas.

A Table, A Garden, And A Courtroom

*Maundy Thursday Service
Including Drama*

Leonard V. Kalkwarf

A Table, A Garden, And A Courtroom

Maundy Thursday Service Including Drama

Production Notes

This is a drama in three acts with five women, sixteen men, and two liturgical dancers. There are speaking parts for one woman and six men.

This drama is preferably done within the context of an evening worship service. Special lighting is necessary to make this effective. Lights must be dimmed several times. A floodlight and two movable spots are required. Having "walking" mikes is an important option for all who have speaking parts.

A long table is placed in the chancel at which the disciples and Jesus are seated in the same manner as in daVinci's famous painting of the Last Supper. From left to right the disciples are: Andrew, James the Lesser, Nathaniel, Judas, Peter, John, Jesus, Thomas, James, Phillip, Matthew, Thaddeus, and Simon.

Following the opening of the service, which begins with a Call To Worship and a Hymn, the sanctuary is in darkness with just enough light to be able to see people walking up the aisles.

Four women, dressed in long black robes and headdresses, each with a large basket in her hand, gather in the back of the sanctuary.

Disciples and Jesus gather in an adjoining room and assume proper position in line for entering chancel. Judas and Jesus have walking mikes; table mike to be used by Peter and is "open" most of the time so that the background conversation of the disciples can be heard.

Pilate and Claudia enter into the left transept after the sanctuary is darkened.

Sometime during the service, the two Temple Guards gather in the narthex, later to be joined by Judas.

Characters

Disciples — Judas and Peter have speaking roles, rest are nonspeaking
Jesus
Temple Guard 1
Temple Guard 2
Pilate
Claudia
Choir
Table Setters — four females, nonspeaking
Liturgical Dancers — two, nonspeaking

A Table, A Garden, And A Courtroom

Call To Worship

Leader: One who loves us to the end has invited us here.
We are guests at the table of Jesus Christ.

People: **We come to this memorial feast in gratitude;**
we honor Christ's invitation above all others.

Leader: At this table, we know cleansing and forgiveness.
We are empowered here to live as Christ's disciples.

People: **We are awed that our Savior has chosen us;**
we are embarrassed that Christ would wash our feet.

Leader: Through the broken bread and the cup of blessing,
we participate in the new life Christ offers us.

People: **We reach out for the gifts that Jesus offers;**
we seek to pass them on in Jesus' name.

Hymn   "Love Divine, All Loves Excelling"
(Choir processes up center aisle and goes to south transept where they remain for the entire service. The liturgical dancers follow the choir and sit in the first pew.)

Act 1 — A Table

Scene 1 — Setting Of The Table By Four Women
(There is organ music and all the lights are on low until the women are seated in their pew. Two enter by the side aisles [one right, one left] and two by the center aisle. The women go slowly but immediately to the table, which already has a white tablecloth on it. They set the table with the items as found in Leonardo da Vinci's painting. After setting table they move to the front pew in front of pulpit and remain there for the rest of the service. All lights go off.)

Scene 2 — Disciples Assume Positions At Table
(Entering from the adjoining room in darkness, the disciples and Jesus assume the same pose as in da Vinci's painting. When in place, the floodlight comes on and the pose is held for 25 seconds after which only the chancel lights come on. The disciples sit in a relaxed manner.)

Scene 3 — Disciples Converse
(Disciples engage in animated but subdued conversation after which the following conversation is heard.)

Jesus: I have wanted to eat this Passover with you before I have to suffer. After all, I will not be able to do so again until it is fulfilled in the kingdom of God. I do want you to know that one of you is going to betray me.

(Disciples look at each other, wondering who it is, and some asking that of the others.)

Several Disciples: Lord, I would not do that.

Jesus: The one who will do this is the one who has dipped his hand in the bowl with me. How sad. It would have been better for him if he had never been born!

Judas: Teacher, you certainly do not mean me, do you?

Jesus: You said so.

Scene 4 — Jesus Washes Peter's Feet

(Jesus gets up and moves to the front of the table, beckoning to John, the first disciple on his right, to come. Jesus takes off his outer robe and ties a towel around himself. Then he pours water into a basin and begins to wash John's feet. He then beckons to Thomas, the first disciple on his left, and washes his feet; then Peter, who is the second disciple on his right.)

Peter: Lord, are you going to wash my feet?

Jesus: You do not know now what I am doing, but later you will understand.

Peter: You will never wash my feet!

Jesus: Unless I wash you, you have no share with me.

Peter: Lord, not my feet only but also my hands and my head!

Jesus: One who has bathed does not need to wash, except for the feet, but is entirely clean. And you are clean, though not all of you.

(At this point, Judas picks up his money bag and quietly gets up and exits by way of a side door where he remains just outside the doorway.)

Scene 5 — Jesus Institutes The Lord's Supper

(Jesus returns to a sitting position at the table after washing Peter's feet.)

Jesus: Do you understand what I have done? If I, as your Lord and Teacher, wash your feet, then you should wash one another's feet. I have set an example for you. You are to serve one another.

(Jesus takes bread.)

Jesus: Take, eat, this is my body.

(The disciples all break off and eat a piece of bread. Jesus takes a chalice.)

Jesus: Drink from it, all of you; for this is the blood of the covenant, which is poured out for many for the forgiveness of sins. I tell you, I will never again drink of this fruit of the vine until that day when I drink it new with you in my Father's kingdom.

(The disciples all drink from a chalice.)

(The lights go out slowly and Judas slips back into position; the flood comes on and the disciples hold the pose as in the painting for about 25 seconds; the flood goes out and the disciples take a relaxed position as the regular lights come on with secondary brightness.)

Scene 6 — Choir And Liturgical Dancers
(The Choir is seated in and sings "Come To The Table" from the left transept. The Liturgical Dancers dance in front of the table.)

Scene 7 — Communion Is Served
(Disciples take the bread and distribute it to the people. This is most effective if not done in a highly organized manner. Some of the disciples are wearing sandals while others are barefoot. Worshipers are to break off a piece of bread and hold it. Disciples return to the table and stand in front, facing the table.)

Jesus: Take, eat, this is my body.

(Disciples take the trays with the cup from a table off to the side and distribute to the people. Disciples return to the table and stand in front, facing the table.)

Jesus: This is my blood of the covenant poured out for many.

(Following the serving of the Lord's Supper, the lights go out. Judas exits quickly and makes his way in the dark to the narthex to join the Temple Guards who have previously assembled there. Jesus, Peter, James, and John go to the right transept where the garden scene will take place. The rest of the disciples sit in the pews in the left transept opposite the Choir.)

Act 2 — A Garden

Scene 1 — Garden Scene
(All lights remain out. A spot is now focused on the garden setting. The garden scene should be elevated, perhaps with the use of choir risers, and surrounded by plants, such as potted palms left from Palm Sunday. Jesus is not visible. Peter, James, and John are in sleeping positions. The place remains quiet for thirty to sixty seconds.)

Scene 2 — Jesus Approaches The Sleeping Disciples
Jesus: Could you not stay awake for one hour?

(Jesus moves toward center of the garden risers and there kneels while Peter, James, and John continue sleeping.)

Jesus: My Father, if it is possible, let this cup pass from me; yet not what I want but what you want.

(*Jesus gets up and walks toward the sleeping disciples.*)

Jesus: Are you still sleeping and taking your rest? See, the hour is at hand, and the Son of Man is betrayed into the hands of sinners. Get up. My betrayer is coming.

(*The spotlight continues to shine on the garden. A commotion is heard coming from the center aisle of the sanctuary.*)

Scene 3 — Judas And The Temple Guards
(*When Judas, who is about fifteen feet ahead of the guards, gets near the front of nave, he stops and faces the Temple Guards who have stopped and are now standing in the center aisle.*)

Temple Guard 1: I thought you were going to bring us to the Rabbi!

(*There is a pause before Temple Guard 2 speaks.*)

Temple Guard 2: You mean you don't know where he is?

(*Judas looks toward the garden and then turns and looks down the center aisle and speaks to the Temple Guards.*)

Judas: Wait a minute. Yes, just as I thought! He went to his favorite place, Gethsemane. Follow me and I will take you to him.

(*Temple Guards catch up to Judas and follow him to the garden.*)

Scene 4 — Judas Betrays Jesus With A Kiss
Judas: Greetings, rabbi!

(*Having said that, Judas embraces Jesus with a kiss.*)

Jesus: Friend, do what you are here to do.

(*Jesus turns to the congregation, as if speaking to a mob.*)

Jesus: Have you come out here with swords and clubs to arrest me as though I were a bandit? Every day I sat in the temple teaching and you did not arrest me.

(*Judas, Peter, James, and John go rushing across the front of the sanctuary to the south transept.*)

Act 3 — A Courtroom

Scene 1 — The Courtroom

(Lights remain out and the spot on the garden goes out. A spot comes on and is focused on the courtroom setting. This is an elevated platform, perhaps made of choir risers, from which Pilate and Claudia will be speaking. Pilate is standing ready to speak. He is dressed as a Roman Governor. Claudia is standing in the shadows and is not visible. Pilate speaks to the congregation as a man of authority.)

Pilate: I am Roman. I am proud of the greatness of my country.

And I am the governor of Judea. I am the procurator of the entire region that includes Samaria and Judea extending from Caesarea on the Mediterranean in the north as far south as Gaza and the Dead Sea. My authority is supreme. I have absolute and complete rule of this entire area except over Roman citizens who are directly responsible to Rome.

I am indebted to one person for my career success — my wife, Claudia.

You would love her. She is young. She is vivacious. She is beautiful. She is the granddaughter of Caesar Augustus, the ruler during the years of Jesus' birth and boyhood. She has royal blood and is well educated. She has had all the cultural advantages of Rome. She knows her way around the best people.

When I was ready to take a new assignment, she convinced the necessary bureaucratic heads to make a place for me. A ruler was never permitted to take his wife on assignment when sent to a hardship post like this one. But leave it to Claudia. She managed. Not that I minded, though at times she does cramp my style.

Claudia is such a *sensitive* person. She is also very religious. It's difficult to live with a sensitive, religious person when you are trying to get ahead in this world, especially when sometimes you have to wink at certain practices and use a little muscle to accomplish your goals.

Jerusalem isn't exactly a picnic. It has a reputation of getting out of hand at festival times such as during Passover. It has a carnival atmosphere, like the Philadelphia Mummers on New Year's Day or the Mardi Gras in New Orleans. That was the situation back in 26 A.D. And it was the death of my career. Because of it, you call my name to remembrance whenever you recite together your historic Apostles' Creed.

I have replayed that event in my mind over and over and over again.

Join me as I relive that event once more.

(Claudia enters from the south transept and stands by Pilate.)

Pilate: Claudia, what are you doing up so early? It's only 6 o'clock in the morning.

Claudia: Pilate, I have had a terrible night's sleep. In fact, I hardly slept at all.

Pilate: Why, what is the matter?

Claudia: I realize you are not aware that I overheard your conversation last night when the high priest, Caiaphas, came over to talk to you. This whole thing with the Nazarene is rigged from start to finish. Caiaphas told you everything, how Judas, one of the followers would tip off the guards, they would arrest him, bring him to you and after a quick trial, he would be sentenced.

Please don't do that. He is somebody special. Now that we are so far from Rome, the gods of Rome are of little comfort to me. And this man seems so different.

Pilate: Claudia, my dear. You are so sensitive. Forget about what you heard last night. I have to do this. I am so indebted to this shrewd high priest. Besides, what difference does it make? This man from Nazareth has created a lot of commotion among his people.

(Claudia leaves with the spotlight on the courtroom but the other spotlight also comes on shining on the garden where the guards each take Jesus by the arm and begin walking toward the court with the spotlight shining on them. Jesus' head is bowed.)

Pilate: Look at me. Tell me something, "Are you the king of the Jews?"

Jesus: Well, that is what you say. My kingdom is not of this world. If my kingdom were from this world, my followers would be fighting to keep me from being handed over to the Jews. But as it is, my kingdom is not from here.

Pilate: So, you are a king?

Jesus: You say that I am a king. For this I was born, and for this I came into the world to testify to the truth. Everyone who belongs to the truth listens to my voice.

Pilate: What is truth? Yes, tell me, what is truth? *(lengthy pause)* I want you to know that the chief priest has accused you of many things. I cannot believe he made up these charges, especially since I know you have stirred up a lot of people.

(Jesus continues to look down with head slightly bowed while the Temple Guards continue to hold his arms, one on each side.)

Pilate: Look at me. Don't you have an answer for all of these accusations? Are you just going to stand there and not defend yourself?

(Claudia enters and stands close to Pilate.)

Pilate: Claudia, my dear, why did you come here?

Claudia: Pilate, please, have nothing to do with this man. I had a dream last night and it was awful. I dreamt that if you went through with this, if you found him guilty, if you sentenced him, you would never be at peace with yourself again. Please, for my sake, don't do it. Don't let Caiaphas manipulate you in this way.

Pilate: It's too late now!

Claudia: No, it is not! The Jews have a practice that you can release somebody from prison. Why don't you do that? Jesus will go free and you will have peace of mind.

(There is a lengthy pause.)

Pilate: Hmm, you know you may be right! Maybe that is what I ought to do. I want you all to know that I find no fault with this man, and as it is your custom, I will release a prisoner today. I know it is out of jealousy that the chief priest brought Jesus to me. So, I ask you, do you want me to release for you the king of the Jews?

Choir: No! No! Barabbas! Barabbas! Barabbas!

Pilate: But I find no fault with this man! What evil has he done? What is it that you want me to do with him who is called the king of the Jews?

Choir: Crucify him! Crucify him! Crucify him!

Pilate: Very well then, as you wish. After all, he is your king. Let everyone see that he claims to be a king.

(Temple Guards place on the head of Jesus a crown of thorns and place a purple robe over his shoulders. Then they take Jesus, each by the arm and walk with him down the center aisle, in darkness and into the narthex, during which the spot continues to be on Pilate and Claudia.)

Pilate: I am innocent of this man's blood. You are responsible for his death, not me.

(Pilate washes his hands in a symbolic way and takes a towel and dries them. The spot goes out and there is now total darkness and remains so until after the Benediction is given.)

Subdued Organ Music

(Jesus, Disciples, Choir, Liturgical Dancers, Temple Guards, and Table Setters exit by a back door, leaving the mood created by this drama.)

Benediction
Tomorrow and Sunday, the worst and the best will take place. Go in peace, serve the Lord, for he has done great and marvelous things for you.

(The lights come on slowly but not to full brightness. The people leave.)

It Seems Like Just Yesterday!

*Good Friday Service Of
Remembrance For Jesus Christ*

Pamela D. Williams

It Seems Like Just Yesterday!

Introduction

When I was a child during the early '60s, stores and businesses closed on Good Friday afternoon. Churches held services from noon until 3 p.m. as a way to remember Jesus suffering on the cross. In this age of 24/7 consumer convenience, stores and businesses rarely close and churches find the attendance at Good Friday afternoon services dwindling.

The purpose of this service is to bring us to a stop, if only for a few minutes, on Good Friday. In an effort to provide an opportunity for solemn reflection despite busy schedules, this program runs approximately one hour and could be presented over the noon hour. As an evening service, this could be extended to an appropriate length simply by the addition of anthems, solos, or litanies.

A memorial service for Jesus Christ comprises the basic premise of this program. The order of worship follows the standard format of most memorial services found in hymnals today. As is customary at many remembrance services, individuals are asked to share what the deceased has meant to them. How has he impacted your life?

May this service provide a creative avenue for reflection on the influence of Christ's life and suffering, not just on these biblical characters, but on each one of us.

Production Notes

In this service, seven biblical characters (one is anonymous and this part is read by the Leader) share life-changing moments they experienced with Jesus. All seven could be included in the program or you may choose as many or as few as you have time and volunteers to involve. Costumes are optional and can be as simple as a shawl covering the head and shoulders or a man's dark bathrobe over street clothes. Characters may follow the listed order or may be presented in alternative arrangements. In order to ensure that everyone in the audience can hear, each character should make his/her way to a microphone to share their remembrances, or arrange to rent body microphones.

This program employs a Leader to provide smooth transition between the various segments. The Leader's comments may be deleted or expanded as desired. Passages in bold indicate those parts that are to be spoken by the congregation.

The hymns listed are suggestions only. Others that may be more familiar to your audience could easily be substituted.

Characters
> Leader
> Peter
> Mary Magdalene
> The Blind Man
> Mary, the Mother of Jesus
> Nicodemus
> Martha

It Seems Like Just Yesterday!

Worship Service

Introduction

Leader: The focus of a Good Friday service is to remind us of the suffering of our Savior, Jesus Christ. The problem is, we, as Christians, are Easter people. We already know the end of the story, and we often forget how tragic the day Christ was crucified really was. Today, let us set aside our busyness and pause for a few moments to imagine what that Friday held for the people who lived and walked with Jesus. In doing so, may the Holy Spirit touch our hearts and help us realize the depth of God's sacrificial love for us.

We come together in sorrow, acknowledging our sins and shortcomings. May God grant us his grace, that in our failures we may find forgiveness, in our loss comfort, and in our despair hope.

"God is our refuge and strength, a very present help in trouble. Therefore we will not fear, though the earth should change, though the mountains shake in the heart of the sea; though its waters roar and foam, though the mountains tremble with its tumult. The Lord of hosts is with us; the God of Jacob is our refuge" (Palms 46:1-3, 7).

Please stand and join me in singing the hymn "Faith Of Our Fathers."

Hymn   "Faith Of Our Fathers"

Prayer

Leader: Let us pray together.

People: **Lord, you know everything we do; you understand our thoughts and our feelings. You have been our shelter through all generations. O God, our souls are thirsty for you today. Lift our eyes above the mountains of life, and help us to see your salvation. Grant us your grace and comfort during this hour of reflection. Amen.**

Scripture   Psalm 130:1-5

Leader: Hear these words of David from Psalm 130: "Out of the depths I cry to you, O Lord. Lord, hear my voice! Let your ears be attentive to the voice of my supplications! If you, O Lord, should mark iniquities, Lord, who could stand? But there is forgiveness with you, so that you may be revered. I wait for the Lord, my soul waits, and in his word I hope" (Psalm 130:1-5).

Old Testament Lesson   Isaiah 43:1-5

Leader: Listen to God's words of comfort spoken through the prophet Isaiah: "Do not fear, for I have redeemed you; I have called you by name, you are mine. When you pass through the waters, I will be with you; and through the rivers, they shall not overwhelm you; when you walk through fire you shall not be burned, and the flame shall not consume you. For I am the Lord your God, the Holy One of Israel, your Savior. Because you are precious in my sight, and honored, and I love you, I give people in return for you, nations in exchange for your life. Do not fear, for I am with you" (Isaiah 43:1-5).

New Testament Lesson   2 Corinthians 4:18

Leader: Be encouraged by these words from 2 Corinthians: "We look not at what can be seen but at what cannot be seen; for what can be seen is temporary, but what cannot be seen is eternal" (2 Corinthians 4:18).

Leader: Please stand as we sing "O God, Our Help In Ages Past."

Hymn   "O God, Our Help In Ages Past"

Witnesses

Leader: You may be seated. At this time I would like to invite family and friends to briefly tell how Jesus Christ has touched their lives and what knowing him has meant to them.

(Peter immediately walks boldly to the microphone.)

Peter: My name is Peter, and yes, I knew Jesus ... although just a few nights ago — the awful night he was arrested — I claimed three times that I didn't know him. I still can't believe I did that — after all we have been through together.

My brother, Andrew and I are fishermen by trade ... now fishers of men. One day we were out in the lake working our nets when we noticed a guy standing on the shore watching us. He really seemed to be enjoying himself. After a while, Andrew and I gathered up our nets and waded to shore. We stood talking to the guy for the longest time. We both felt this immediate connection with him! I soon realized that this was no ordinary man. He had such passion and authority! I found him intriguing. You see, I'm a man of passion myself. So when he invited us to join him in his ministry, neither of us hesitated — we both jumped at the chance!

Now I've always been kind of impulsive, but for Andrew to make a snap decision like that — to just up and leave our fishing business to follow this guy — well, I knew something extraordinary was happening! Turned out to be the best decision of my life!

Talk about exciting! Every day we traveled with Jesus as he talked to people, and helped them out. He even healed them! People were delivered from evil spirits that had tortured them for years! It was an amazing time!

But what really touched my heart was Jesus' passion for people to be made holy, to be forgiven of their sins. He wanted them to realize that salvation comes through faith in him. For truly he was the Christ — the Son of the living God!

Jesus showed us what God the Father is really like — loving, merciful, and holy. He made it clear that when we trust in him as our Savior, we belong to God. We are his own people, chosen to proclaim his wonderful acts!

These last three years with Jesus have been awesome, inspiring, and admittedly, at times, terrifying. He really stretched my faith. One time he even had me walk on top of the water with him! Talk about frightening! That awe-filled moment is etched on my mind forever! I remember it like it was just yesterday.

However, not everyone agreed with what Jesus had to say, especially the Jewish authorities and leaders. We faced opposition nearly every day. And it all came to a head the other night in the garden. The authorities seemed to be everywhere. When they dragged Jesus away, the rest of the fellows and I scattered in a dozen different directions. I'm ashamed to admit I acted like a coward. How could I have let him down like that? He gave up his life for me! And I wouldn't even admit I knew him! If only I could tell him how sorry I am.... *(returns to his seat, ruefully shaking his head)*

Leader: Peter reminds us of the words of Jesus when he said, "If you know me, you will know my Father also. From now on you do know him and have seen him ... Whoever has seen me has seen the Father" (John 14:7, 9). Is there someone else who would like to share?

(Mary Magdalene immediately stands and waits until Leader motions for her to come forward.)

Mary Magdalene: My name is Mary Magdalene. When I first met Jesus, I was a tortured and tormented soul, desperate for release. I was loved by no one ... and misunderstood by everyone. I walked a lonely path in life. All my wealth could not buy what I needed most — peace.

But I began hearing stories of a man who could heal the sick and even cast out demons. I wondered — could he possibly help me? Could he set me free from all the evil spirits that haunted me? He had delivered others. I saw it with my own eyes. But could he really deliver me?

Part of me held back. What if he couldn't help me? No one else had been able to. If Jesus couldn't, then I would be bound by the demons forever. I wasn't sure I could face the despair.

Of course the evil in me resisted the idea — if they were cast out, where would they go? None of them wanted to be relegated to roaming the earth to find another host.

But a force stronger than I ever imagined, drew me to him — the force of his love. I felt it even from the back of the crowd. For one brief moment I locked eyes with him. And with just that one look, I felt it — acceptance, mercy, and most of all love — a holy and powerful love for even me — a shunned and feared woman. I dared to hope.

For a while, the multitudes of people pressing around him kept me at bay. But I was irresistibly drawn forward. And with just a word he delivered me! How wonderful to be released from the demons that bound me!

My life changed forever that day. Jesus not only became my Deliverer but he became my Savior! I couldn't get enough of his teaching! A group of us women became friends — genuine friends united by our love for Jesus. We pooled our resources and helped him and his disciples in any way we could.

When word came that Jesus had been arrested, we stared at one another in utter disbelief. We knew that his teachings angered some, but enough to crucify him? No! How could anyone do that to him, the Savior of us all?

My heart feels like it is crushed within me. What can I do for my Savior now? He set me free, but I am powerless to help him.

There is one thing, though, that we women understand — in life or in death we are faithful. Tomorrow Mary, Salome, and I will perform the burial rites that we could not fulfill because of the coming Sabbath. It seems like the least we can do for the one who has done so much for us. *(bows to the leader, and returns to her seat)*

Leader: Thank you, Mary. Jesus promised, "Peace I leave with you; my peace I give to you. I do not give to you as the world gives. Do not let your hearts be troubled, and do not let them be afraid" (John 14:27).

Scripture Psalm 23

Leader: One of the most beloved passages of scripture is the 23rd Psalm. Let us stand together and read this psalm responsively.

Leader: The Lord is my shepherd, I shall not want.

People: **He makes me lie down in green pastures; he leads me beside still waters; he restores my soul.**

Leader: He leads me in right paths for his name's sake.

People: **Even though I walk through the darkest valley, I fear no evil; for you are with me; your rod and your staff — they comfort me.**

Leader: You prepare a table before me in the presence of my enemies; you anoint my head with oil; my cup overflows.

People: **Surely goodness and mercy shall follow me all the days of my life, and I shall dwell in the house of the Lord my whole life long.**

Leader: You may be seated.

(The Blind Man makes his way to the front.)

Leader: I don't believe I know your name, sir, but would you like to go next?

The Blind Man: My name isn't important. What is important is that Jesus, the man we are here to remember, gave me my sight ... and so much more!

You see I was born totally blind. My parents did their best with me, but my blindness made it very difficult for them ... and for me. I really couldn't get a job. No one wanted to even associate with a blind man, let alone hire one. So I did the only thing I could — I begged. Every day I would sit by the side of the road hoping that someone would take pity on me and feel generous. Some days were better than others.

I remember distinctly that Sunday Jesus healed me. I was sitting at my usual place. I heard some people coming. Even though I was blind, I got pretty good at tuning into my other senses. I could tell from the sounds, the vibrations, and the cloud of dust that rolled over me that it was quite a group. They were discussing something — and I got the feeling it centered around me.

I didn't think much about it though ... people often made comments to each other about me as they passed by. But when this group stopped directly in front of me, they had my full attention.

I always braced myself when a big group stopped near me ... I *hoped* they were pausing to pull some money from their pockets, but sometimes ... well, people can be cruel.

Sure enough, one man spit on the ground beside me. I lowered my head and waited for the insults. But instead, he mixed the spit with the dust, and said to his friends, "He is blind that God's power might be seen at work in him." Then he reached over and put his hand on my shoulder. His touch was so gentle — and yet powerful! Oddly, I felt no fear. He took some of the mud and rubbed it on my eyes and said, "Go and wash your face in the pool of Siloam."

I have to admit, it was a strange request, but for some unexplainable reason, I felt compelled to obey him.

Can you imagine the joy and surprise I felt when I opened my eyes after washing my face and found I could see? Let me tell you, I *ran* back to thank the man.

71

But he was gone. Some of my neighbors and a few officials from our synagogue were there. They asked me if Jesus was the one who had healed me. I told them that I really didn't know the man. All I knew was that I was blind and now I could see.

Thankfully, later that day I met Jesus on the road again. I had to tell him that I had done what he said to do and I could see! But more than that, I just had to let him know how he had changed my life! I now felt accepted, productive, and worthwhile!

As we talked, as hard as it is to believe, I learned something that changed my life even more than restoring my sight! My spiritual eyes were opened! All my life I had heard the scriptures about the coming Messiah. At that moment on the road, I suddenly realized that I was face to face with God's promised one! Jesus, the man who healed me, is the Messiah, my Savior! If only I could see him again.... *(turns and walks purposefully back to his seat)*

Leader: Thank you, sir. Remember these words of Jesus: "Do not let your hearts be troubled. Believe in God. Believe also in me. In my Father's house there are many dwelling places. If it were not so, would I have told you that I go to prepare a place for you? And if I go and prepare a place for you, I will come again and will take you to myself, so that where I am, there you may be also" (John 14:1-3). Is there a family member who would like to share?

(Mary, the Mother of Jesus rises and makes her way to the microphone, handkerchief in hand, head bowed. She dabs at her eyes as she speaks.)

Mary, the Mother of Jesus: Excuse my appearance. The last few days have been very difficult for me. You see, I am Mary and Jesus was my own dear son. The sorrow of losing him has broken my heart! It is just as Simeon prophesied in the temple when Jesus was just a tiny baby.

The wonder of being chosen to bear the Son of God has still not worn off, even after 33 years. Though my heart struggles to praise the Lord at this moment, I must focus, not on this tragedy, but on the great things our mighty God has done for us — especially sending our Savior. For you see Jesus, my son, is also the Messiah!

I was told this at the very beginning. I knew I had been given an awesome responsibility, but much of the time I simply loved him as any other mother loves her son. I was very proud of Jesus. He did wonderful healings and miracles for so many. He even helped me out at a family wedding when the wine ran out. I mentioned the problem to Jesus and he turned six large jars of water into the best wine anyone ever tasted!

And his teachings! No one could explain the scriptures quite like my Jesus. His wisdom and insight came straight from his heavenly Father.

Oh, I admit there have been struggles and challenges. Even his own family — even I, often misunderstood Jesus. I'll never forget that time we were returning from the Passover Festival, and Joseph and I had assumed Jesus was traveling with the other boys until he didn't show up for supper. When Joseph returned from searching for Jesus and told me he was nowhere in the camp, I was terrified! It wasn't like him to worry us. I assumed the worst. We retraced our steps to Jerusalem and found Jesus visiting with the priests! Why in the world would he think he could just stay behind and assume we would know where he was? I couldn't understand it. I was just thankful no harm had come to him. How I wish that were true now.

The past three years, Jesus has been completely dedicated to his ministry. He hasn't been home as often as I would have liked, but as he reminded me, he had to be about his heavenly Father's business. He spent a lot of time preaching and explaining the scriptures. He wanted so much for people to believe in him and to find forgiveness.

I guess Jesus' teachings were just too radical, too contrary to the comforts of the old ways for our religious leaders. The last few weeks I have felt the tension mounting.

It seems like just yesterday when the people paved the road with palm branches for my son to travel over. The crowd seemed to finally recognize who he really was! They were even calling him "the king of Israel"! How could they shout, "Crucify him, crucify him," a few days later?

Despite Simeon's prediction and warning, I can't believe anyone actually put my dear son to death. Yet I saw it with my own eyes. I would have collapsed completely if my sister and several friends hadn't been there to hold me up. How can I bear the pain of losing him? He is our Messiah! I, better than anyone else *know* that he is the Son of God! How can he possibly be dead? Forgive me.... I just can't go on. *(covers her face with her handkerchief and hurriedly returns to her seat)*

Prayer

Leader: Could we pause for a moment of prayer?

Lord, we look to you for help at all times. Turn to us and be merciful. We are lonely and weak. Relieve us of our worries and distress and save us from all our troubles. In your constant love and goodness, remember us, O Lord. Amen.

Jesus knows our human frailties and offers us these words of comfort, "I will not leave you orphaned. I am coming to you. In a little while you will no longer see me. Do not let your hearts be troubled and do not let them be afraid. Rejoice that I am going to the Father, because the Father is greater than I" (John 14:18, 19, 27-28).

(As soon as Leader finishes, Nicodemus moves quickly to the microphone. He is carrying a wooden box containing spices and cloths.)

Nicodemus: I would like to speak next, if I may. *(Leader nods permission)* I must soon be on my way to meet a friend of mine.

My name is Nicodemus. As a member of the Pharisees, it is my business to keep apprised of the spiritual climate among our people. Stories of miracles and rumors of overstepping Jewish law began circulating around a man named Jesus. These tales flew thick and fast for quite some time before I decided to check things out for myself. My fellow Pharisees thought the man was at least a con artist and more likely, a blasphemer. I wasn't so sure though. I felt it only fair to get the facts before we condemned him.

Staying in the background to avoid drawing attention to myself, I listened to his teachings on several occasions. I have to admit, he did seem to be sent by God. He spoke with authority and a phenomenal knowledge of scripture.

As a scholar and interpreter of Jewish Law, some of Jesus' statements raised questions in my mind. I wanted to speak with him. Knowing how the other Pharisees felt though, I waited until dark to approach him.

From the very start of our conversation he seemed to be able to see deep into my heart! He cut right to the core of my question. In a few short hours that evening, he taught me much about the kingdom of heaven. He made it plain that being a religious leader did not guarantee I had a reserved place in heaven.

In fact, he said something very odd. "You must be born again." At first I didn't know what he meant. Can you imagine? Me, an expert in the law needing to have a spiritual concept explained! But he patiently helped me understand that my own good works and obedience to the law didn't make me good enough for the kingdom of heaven. I had to believe in him for my salvation!

Jesus told me that God loves the world so much that he was sent in order that anyone, yes, anyone, could be saved just by believing in him! He offers everyone a second chance — a new life! This was extraordinary teaching and differed greatly from our traditional Jewish Law and tradition!

But somehow, deep within me, his words rang true. I mulled them over in my mind for a long time. I secretly shared them with my friend, Joseph, from Arimathea. We discussed Jesus' teachings at length and found new life in his words! We both came to believe Jesus was who he said he was — the Son of God!

Most sadly, the other religious leaders weren't convinced, though. They have done the unthinkable. They had Jesus accused falsely and now he has been crucified!

I spoke with Joseph this afternoon. He has gained permission to bury Jesus in a garden tomb close by Calvary. I bought these spices and cloths to wrap the body in. It will be a bittersweet privilege to serve the Lord Jesus in this way. Thank you.

Leader: Jesus made the way of salvation very clear to all of us when he said, "I am the way, the truth, and the life. No one comes to the Father except through me" (John 14:6). At this time I would like to share a letter that was delivered to me just before the service started. For reasons that will become obvious, the writer wishes to remain anonymous.

(reads from letter) To the gathered faithful, I apologize for not being able to attend in person, but I am a Roman Army Officer and my commander would have my head if I attended a service in memory of Jesus. He thinks the man caused enough trouble when he was alive. But somehow, I feel the truth needs to be known so I sent this letter by way of one of my subordinates.

In the governor's office you hear all kinds of news and rumors. People are always coming in to report on this and that — sometimes for the good of Rome and sometimes for their own gain. The religious element in Jerusalem has been a repeated source of contention for Governor Pilate. This morning they barely waited for daylight before bothering him with more of their religious arguments.

Lately we have been hearing numerous reports about this man Jesus, whom you are here to remember today. Stories of healings and miracles connected with him were circulating everywhere. In fact, the servant of one of my fellow officers has supposedly been healed. They say Jesus didn't even touch him! He simply said it would be done and it was! He is a man who seems to wield much authority.

But the religious leaders see him as a threat to them. They say his teachings are contrary to their religious law. Some even say he claims to be the Son of God! This morning they accused him of trying to overthrow Rome and become king of the Jews — an accusation not taken lightly by government officials.

In many ways I wish I had not been on duty this morning. Overseeing crucifixions is a horrific assignment. And yet, at the same time, the events of this day have been life changing.

I was on duty at the palace when these religious authorities brought Jesus in. He neither looked nor acted like a criminal. All through the interrogation and sentencing he barely said a word. It was a humiliating and brutal process. Pilate ultimately gave the order for him to be crucified alongside two thieves.

I have witnessed my share of crucifixions, but this man was different. He refused to fight back. And even when he was in agony, he showed such selflessness and mercy! I've never seen anything like it. Why, he told one of the thieves hanging beside him that he would see him in paradise today!

I have to admit it was a very scary time. The crowd was an ugly mix — some were angry, some sorrowful, and some almost gleeful. The sky got very dark and we heard a thunderous rumbling. I thought a bad storm had come up, but when the rocks around us split open, I knew it was an earthquake. Suddenly Jesus cried out something I couldn't understand and when I looked up, he was dead.

For me it was like time stood still. In that moment I realized with horror what we had done. We had crucified the Son of God! As I bowed my head in shame, ever so gently the words he spoke as we nailed him to the cross echoed through my mind. "Father, forgive them, they don't know what they are doing." Forgiveness. He offered forgiveness to even the likes of me. *(pauses as this is the end of letter)*

Amen. We thank the Lord that each of us can receive God's forgiveness. Jesus told us, "There is joy in the presence of the angels of God over one sinner who repents" (Luke 15:10). We have time for just one more person to share. *(Martha raises hand)* Yes, ma'am. Please come to the front.

(Martha comes to the front.)

Martha: My name is Martha and Jesus was a close friend of mine ... of our whole family really ... and we loved one another just like family.

Jesus spent a good bit of time in our home. He knew he was welcome anytime he got near Bethany. He sat at our table and shared our meals on more than one occasion. I always looked forward to his visits because of what he brought to the table — not fresh fruit or a bottle of good wine, but rich spiritual food!

I remember one afternoon in particular. Jesus and his disciples stopped by our village after doing some teaching nearby. They were tired and hungry. Jesus knew I would take good care of them. My sister, Mary, sat down and talked with Jesus while I started preparations for the meal. I figured she would come help me after some polite chitchat, but she just sat there listening!

I have to admit I was getting pretty frustrated with her! It's not easy to get a meal ready for thirteen hungry people! I could have really used her help!

But when I mentioned it to Jesus, he set me in my place. Told me I needed to get my priorities straight! He was never one to mince words.

But neither am I.

He was right, of course. I fuss too much about earthly things when it's the godly things that matter. And I'm trying to work on that, although I did notice a cobweb up above that light fixture, pastor. *(points up at light)*

Anyway, back to Jesus. Without a doubt, the most important lesson Jesus taught me was when my brother Lazarus got very sick and died. I remember that time so well. It seems like it was just yesterday. We had sent Jesus a message, letting him know that Lazarus was ill. We hoped he would come and heal him. But our brother passed away before Jesus got there.

When Jesus arrived, Mary and I talked with him about Lazarus. I told him plainly that if he had been there, Lazarus wouldn't have died! He reminded us that he himself is the resurrection and the life and that all who believed in him would live again. Lazarus, Mary, and I already believed Jesus is the Messiah! And we knew that the dead would rise on the last day. At the time, I figured maybe he was just trying to comfort Mary and me.

When Jesus asked where Lazarus was buried we assumed he wanted to pay his respects, so we showed him the tomb. But when he ordered that it be opened, I just had to speak up. For heaven's sake, Lazarus had been dead for four days! The smell would be terrible!

But Jesus simply said, "Didn't I tell you that you would see God's glory if you believed?" And then after a little prayer, he shouted to Lazarus to come out.

Well, let me tell you that my knees buckled when my brother came stumbling out of that tomb! Jesus actually raised him from the dead! Lazarus is alive! And, I for one will never question Jesus again. No matter how bad things may seem, we can always trust him. What he says goes!

And you know, because of that, somehow I just can't quite believe that even death on that horrible cross can keep Jesus down. I think there is more to this story.... *(wanders back to her seat, staring thoughtfully)*

Leader: Thank you, Martha. I know that many more here would like to have shared but often times in situations like these our hearts are just too full and words too inadequate. So now let us draw comfort from the words Jesus spoke in his Sermon on the Mount: "Blessed are the poor in spirit, for theirs is the kingdom of heaven. Blessed are those who mourn, for they will be comforted. Blessed are the meek, for they will inherit the earth. Blessed are those who hunger and thirst for righteousness, for they will be filled. Blessed are the merciful, for they will receive mercy. Blessed are the pure in heart, for they will see God. Blessed are the peacemakers, for they will be called children of God. Blessed are those who are persecuted for righteousness' sake, for theirs is the kingdom of heaven."

Please stand and sing with me our closing hymn, "Hymn Of Promise."

Hymn   "Hymn Of Promise"

Prayer

Leader: I would like to close the service with this prayer from Ephesians chapter 3. According to the riches of his glory, God may grant that you may be strengthened in your inner being with power through his Spirit, and that Christ may dwell in your hearts through faith, as you are being rooted and grounded in love. I pray that you may have the power to comprehend, with all the saints, what is the breadth and length and height and depth, and to know the love of Christ that surpasses knowledge, so that you may be filled with all the fullness of God. Now to him who by the power at work within us is able to accomplish abundantly far more than all we can ask or imagine, to him be glory in the church and in Christ Jesus to all generations, forever and ever. Amen.

Go in peace.

Faces

Good Friday Drama

Michelle Griep

Faces

Good Friday Drama

Characters

Biblical character	Counterpart
Judas	Contemporary Woman
Roman Guard	Teenager
Caiaphas	Businessman
Herod	Elementary Student
Barabbas	Contemporary Person

Notes

Judas represents the pew-warmer, the church attendee who plays the part of a Christian and does it well, but is really only a spectator. Counterpart is Contemporary Woman.

The Roman Guard represents those who sneer at God, those who believe religion is a crutch, outmoded, and outdated. Counterpart is Teenager.

Caiaphas represents the calculated, corporate ladder-climber who will indulge a little bit of Jesus for tolerance sake, but not a lot — especially if it gets in the way of career. Counterpart is Businessman.

Herod represents the thrill seekers, the MTV crowd, the young who crave entertainment at every moment. Counterpart is Elementary Student.

Barabbas represents us all — sinners who deserve eternal damnation. Counterpart is a sobbing, repentant, Contemporary Person.

Setting

Judas, Roman Guard, Caiaphas, Herod, and Barabbas all stand facing the audience. Directly behind, back to back, is their contemporary counterpart. On the floor, at the Roman Guard's feet, have some plastic wrap taped down for him to spit on.

(spotlight on Judas)

Judas: Whenever he spoke, I was there. I was right there. Never missed a sermon. I sat through 'em all.

I knew what he looked like. I could tell you how his eyes sparked when he spoke of hypocrites.

I knew what he sounded like, the way compassion changed his voice to a throaty croak that day a woman mopped his feet with tears.

I even knew the smell of him, overheated, sweaty after a long day's journey between villages. I knew him all right, knew all about him, but ... I didn't *know* him. I played the part of a disciple, but God help me!

I called him Master the very night I betrayed him. I called him Master, Lord, Teacher ... but I never really knew him.

Do you? *(trades places with person behind so that Contemporary Woman is facing out to audience and Judas faces backstage)*

(spotlight on Roman Guard)

Roman Guard: Some said he was the Son of God. Which God? Jupiter? Apollo? God. *(spits on floor)* There is no God.

God is for the weak-minded, those who cannot, or will not, think for themselves. God is for old people, too stubborn, too close minded to consider new ways and new ideas.

Well, I gave 'em a God that day. Me and all the palace guards, we gave 'em a God all right. A heavy scarlet robe to rub against the ripped skin of his back, and a scepter of roughened wood barbed with splinters for his hand.

But the crowning touch, so to speak, was my idea. My own hands were bloodied by the time I fashioned a wreath of thorns and forced it on his head, tearing open fresh trails of blood that ran the length of his forehead. Hah! A God who bleeds.

He was no God. There is no God. And don't you try to tell me there is. *(trades places with person behind so that Teenager is facing out to audience and Roman Guard faces backstage)*

(spotlight on Caiaphas)

Caiaphas: Of course he needed to be taken out. He was bad for business. The people were starting to listen, seek his counsel, quote his words. No, no, no. That would never do for business.

He gave whatever he had, all that he had, to the poor and needy. What kind of business is that? Sinners deserve what God deals to them.

And then there was that whole scene in the temple. Casting money about as if it held no value — gold coins mind you. What a waste.

But when he claimed to be the Son of God, the Messiah. Well, no one usurps my authority. A high priest can, and should, be all that the name implies — there is none higher than me. I've earned my title. I've a right to all the respect and wealth that I've worked so hard for.

It was nothing personal, mind you. Just business. Business that had to be taken care of. You do see that, don't you? *(trades places with person behind so that Businessman is facing out to audience and Caiaphas faces backstage)*

(spotlight on Herod)

Herod: I couldn't wait to see Jesus. As king of Galilee, I'd heard so much about him — water transformed into wine, lepers with new skin, soft and pink as my own. And the women he attracted. Women of ill repute. Jeweled and scented and — let's just say I wouldn't mind a gaggle of those women following after me.

But I digress, ahhhh, yes the miracles. The wonders. Storms at sea stopped by a word from his lips, sight given to those with blind eyes, and even life breathed into those who were dead. Yes, dead! Imagine.

I heard all these stories, day after day, week after week, and I could hardly wait to see the show he'd perform when he finally came to my palace. I love to be entertained. I need to be entertained.

But he stood silent. Quiet. A skinny Jew, lacking any shine or luster. I honestly don't understand what all the fuss was about. Nothing flashy. Nothing fun. Nothing, well, entertaining I suppose.

Why would I give him a second thought when the pleasures of this world are so much more exciting? Why would you? *(trades places with person behind so that Elementary Student is facing out to audience and Herod faces backstage)*

(spotlight on Barabbas)

Barabbas: I should have died that day. It should have been me up on that hill. Me hanging on that cross, not him.

I've done things that innocent men could never even think of. I stirred disillusion and discontent. I lied. I cursed. I hated. I murdered with my words long before I murdered with my hands. I am the guilty one.

That man out there, that Jesus, he didn't do anything. He didn't deserve that kind of humiliation. They spat on him, and they ... they beat him. I mean, they beat him! He could barely stand, his face unrecognizable. Swollen, purple, bloody. I can only wonder at the pain, the unbearable, unending pain.

Why? Why did he have to die? It should've been me I tell you. I should be damned to hell! Do you hear me?

It should have been me. Father, I am sorry. I am so, so sorry. Against you have I sinned, we have all sinned. Forgive me. Your Son's blood is upon my head.

(Barabbas steps aside. Contemporary Person turns around to face audience, then falls to the floor sobbing. Barabbas places his hand on the repentant Contemporary Person briefly, glances back across the stage at all the others still standing there, then turns to audience.)

Barabbas: It should have been us. We all had a hand in his death.

(all exit)

Extinguished

Good Friday Tenebrae (Shadows) Service

Anne W. Anderson

Extinguished

Worship Service

Introduction

Almost 2,000 years ago, Good Friday seemingly extinguished the light of Christ come into the world. This service recalls that sense of emptiness by beginning (after an opening hymn and one or more pastoral reflections) in darkness. Candles are lit as passages about Jesus, the light of the world, are read from John's gospel. Then the focus turns to the seven last words spoken from the cross, and the candles are extinguished, returning the area to darkness.

Running Time

This service takes 30 to 75 minutes depending on the length of the pastoral reflection(s) and whether or not optional choral anthems are used.

Worship Notes

This service is written for nine readers, but can be adapted for as few as two. Readers should represent, if possible, different ages (elementary-age children through senior adults), genders, and ethnic backgrounds. The readings break sentences into fragments, each fragment being read by a different voice, to provide interest, to emphasize various words, and to convey a sense that the scriptures apply to each of us and are not limited to any one age or gender or nationality. Readers should practice together until the sentences flow smoothly. When words are repeated, each reader should vary the emphasis. For additional effect, position readers in different places throughout the sanctuary. The Leader can be one of the pastoral staff or one of the readers. The terms Men, Women, and All refer to the entire congregation. A sample bulletin is included with these parts written out. The silences allow people to absorb the scriptures. They are very important parts of the service and should not be rushed. Allow at least one full minute for each silence.

Setting

Seven candles are arranged across the front of the church — on the altar or spaced across the altar rail. An acolyte holding a lit taper stands with his/her back to the congregation. As the scriptures are read during the first half of the service, the acolyte lights the appropriate candle. During the second half of the service, the acolyte extinguishes each candle. Alternatively, the candles may be placed throughout the sanctuary and a separate acolyte assigned to light/extinguish each candle. Because of the darkness, the readers and choir (if there is one) may need individual book lights or will need to memorize their lines/music. If the words to the songs or responses are projected onto screens, use dark backgrounds and gray or light purple lettering.

(At the beginning of the service, the house lights are up. Any announcements, welcoming statements, and opening prayers that are standard to a particular church should take place here before moving into the rest of the service.)

Opening Hymn   "Were You There When They Crucified My Lord?" (vv. 1 and 2)

Pastoral Reflections On Good Friday
Possible topics include:
- Jesus in the Garden of Gethsemane / Obedient unto death
    Suggested scripture helps: Luke 22:39-53; 1 Corinthians 2:2-8; Hebrews 5:5-9
- What is good about Good Friday? / Redemption
    Suggested scripture helps: Luke 22:54—23:56; Romans 5:6—6:10; Colossians 1:15-23
- It is finished / The final sacrifice
    Suggested scripture helps: John 19; Hebrews 9-10; 1 Peter 1:21-25

Optional Choral Anthem

Leader: The rest of this service will begin and end in darkness. The darkness at the beginning symbolizes both the nothingness prior to creation and the spiritual darkness we all are in before we allow God's light to shine in us and through us. The darkness at the end recalls the darkness of that day almost 2,000 years ago when it appeared that God's light — Jesus — had been put out forever. For safety's sake, the ushers will not admit anyone into the sanctuary while it is dark. Because the lighting will be dim throughout, please do not move around. Keep your children with you. At the end of the service, please wait until the lights are brought back up before leaving. Please remain in the sanctuary in prayer as long as you like. When you leave, please leave in silence.

(House lights are turned off. One acolyte enters holding a lit taper, and stands in front of the candles turned away from the congregation.)

The Light Comes

Reader 1: In the beginning the Word already existed; the Word was with God, and the Word was God. From the very beginning the Word was with God.

Reader 2: Through him God made all things; not one thing in all creation was made without him.

Reader 3: The Word was the source of life, and this life brought light *(acolyte lights first candle)* to people.

Reader 2: The light shines in the darkness, and the darkness has never put it out (John 1:1-5).

Reader 1: The Word was in the world, and though God made the world through him, yet the world did not recognize him.

Reader 3: He came to his own country, but his own people did not receive him.

Reader 2: Some, however, did receive him and believed in him; so he gave them the right to become God's children. They did not become God's children by natural means, that is by being born as the children of a human father; God himself was their father.

86

Reader 3: The Word became a human being

Reader 2: and full of grace and truth, he lived among us. We saw his glory,

Reader 1: the glory which he received as the Father's only Son (John 1:10-14).

Reader 4: This was the real light *(acolyte lights second candle)* — the light that comes into the world and shines on all people (John 1:9).

Reader 5: "I am the light *(acolyte lights third candle)* of the world," Jesus said. "Whoever follows me will have the light of life and will never walk in darkness" (John 8:12).

Reader 6: Jesus said, "As long as it is day, we must do the work of him who sent me; night is coming when no one can work. While I am in the world, I am the light *(Acolyte lights fourth candle)* for the world" (John 9:45).

Reader 7: Jesus said, "... Those who walk in broad daylight do not stumble, for they see the light *(acolyte lights fifth candle)* of this world. But if they walk during the night they stumble, because they have no light" (John 11:9-10).

Reader 8: Jesus said, "The light will be among you a little longer. Continue on your way while you have the light, so that the darkness will not come upon you; for the one who walks in the dark does not know where he is going. Believe in the light *(acolyte lights sixth candle)*, then, while you have it, so that you will be the people of the light" (John 12:35-36).

Reader 9: Jesus said in a loud voice, "Whoever believes in me believes not only in me but also in him who sent me. Whoever sees me sees also him who sent me.

Reader 8: I have come into the world as light *(acolyte lights seventh candle)*, so that everyone who believes in me should not remain in the darkness.

Reader 7: If people hear my message

Reader 9: and do not obey it

Reader 7: I will not judge them.

Reader 8: I came, not to judge the world, but to save it.

Reader 9: Those who reject me and do not accept my message have one who will judge them.

Reader 7: The words I have spoken

Reader 8: will be their judge on the last day!" (John 12:44-48).

Reader 1: Jesus said, "This is how the judgment works: the light

Reader 2: the light has come

Reader 3: has come into the world

Reader 2: but people love the darkness

Reader 1: rather than the light

Reader 2: because their deeds

Reader 3: their deeds are evil.

Reader 2: Those who do evil things hate the light

Reader 1: and will not come to the light

Reader 3: because they do not want their evil deeds to be shown up" (John 3:18-20).

Hymn   "Were You There When They Crucified My Lord?" (vv. 3 and 4)

Men: Then the Roman soldiers with their commanding officer and the Jewish guards arrested Jesus, tied him up, and took him first to Annas. He was the father-in-law of Caiaphas, who was the high priest that year. It was Caiaphas who had advised the Jewish authorities that it was better that one man should die for all the people (John 18:12-14).

Women: Early in the morning, Jesus was taken from Caiaphas' house to the governor's palace. ... Then Pilate took Jesus and had him whipped. The soldiers made a crown of thorny branches and put it on his head; then they put a purple robe on him and came to him and said, "Long live the King of the Jews!" and they went up and slapped him. ... Then Pilate handed Jesus over to them to be crucified (John 18:28; 19:1-3, 16a).

All: So they took charge of Jesus. He went out, carrying his cross, and came to "The Place of the Skull," as it is called. (In Hebrew it is called "Golgotha.") There they crucified him, and they also crucified two other men, one on each side, with Jesus between them (John 19:16b-18).

Optional Choral Anthem   "For God So Loved The World"

Silence

First Word
Reader 1: Jesus said, "Forgive them, Father! They don't know what they are doing" (Luke 23:34a).
(acolyte extinguishes seventh candle)

All: Father, your Word says that you pity me the way a father pities his children. You know what I am made of; you remember that I am dust. Forgive me, Father, I truly don't know the full extent of anything I do (Psalm 103:13).

Silence

Second Word

Reader 2: One of the criminals hanging there hurled insults at him: "Aren't you the Messiah? Save yourself and us!"

Reader 3: The other one, however, rebuked him, saying, "Don't you fear God? You received the same sentence he did. Ours however, is only right, because we are getting what we deserve for what we did; but he has done no wrong." And he said to Jesus, "Remember me, Jesus, when you come as king!"

Reader 1: Jesus said to him, "I promise you that today you will be in paradise with me" (Luke 23:39-43). *(acolyte extinguishes sixth candle)*

All: Thank you, Father, that it is never too late for me to cry out to you and to be accepted fully by you. Forgive me for the times I am too proud to admit my sin. Help me to turn to you.

Silence

Third Word

Reader 4: Standing close to Jesus' cross were his mother; his mother's sister, Mary, the wife of Clopas; and Mary Magdalene. Jesus saw his mother and the disciple he loved standing there

Reader 1: so he said to his mother, "He is your son." Then he said to the disciple, "She is your mother."

Reader 4: From that time the disciple took her to live in his home (John 19:25-27). *(acolyte extinguishes fifth candle)*

All: In the middle of all your suffering, you thought of others. Forgive me, Jesus, for being so wrapped up in myself and my concerns that I ignore those around me.

Silence

Fourth Word

Reader 5: At noon, the whole country was covered with darkness, which lasted for three hours. At about three o'clock Jesus cried out with a loud shout,

Reader 1: *"Eli, Eli lema sabachthani?"* which means, "My God, my God, why did you abandon me?" (Matthew 27:45-46). *(acolyte extinguishes fourth candle)*

All: Jesus, your word says that you know completely and totally what it is like to be a human being. You know — more than I do — what abandonment feels like. Thank you for becoming a human being, for living on this earth, and for dying a real death.

Silence

Fifth Word

Reader 6: Jesus knew that by now everything had been completed; and in order to make the scripture come true, he said,

Reader 1: "I am thirsty" (John 19:28). *(acolyte extinguishes third candle)*

Women: You promise to give us living water

Men: yet you thirsted.

All: And when you said you were thirsty, they gave you — the creator of all — cheap wine ... vinegar to drink. You thirst for me, and I offer you — my creator, my redeemer, my life — cheap wine ... vinegar.

Silence

Sixth Word

Reader 7: Jesus drank the wine and said,

Reader 1: "It is finished" (John 19:30). *(acolyte extinguishes second candle)*

Silence

Seventh Word

Reader 8: It was about twelve o'clock when the sun stopped shining

Reader 9: and darkness covered the whole country until three o'clock;

Reader 8: and the curtain hanging in the temple was torn in two.

Reader 9: Jesus cried out in a loud voice,

Reader 1: "Father! In your hands I place my spirit!"

Reader 8: He said this

Reader 9: and died (John 23:44-45). *(acolyte extinguishes first candle)*

Depart in silence

Extinguished

Sample Bulletin

Welcome

Hymn   "Were You There When They Crucified My Lord?" (vv. 1 and 2)

Pastoral Reflections And Prayer

Leader: The rest of this service will begin and end in darkness. The darkness at the beginning symbolizes both the nothingness prior to creation and the spiritual darkness we all are in before we allow God's light to shine in us and through us. The darkness at the end recalls the darkness of that day almost 2,000 years ago when it appeared that God's light — Jesus — had been put out forever. For safety's sake, the ushers will not admit anyone into the sanctuary while it is dark. Because the lighting will be dim throughout, please do not move around. Keep your children with you. At the end of the service, please wait until the lights are brought back up before leaving. Please remain in the sanctuary in prayer as long as you like. When you leave, please leave in silence. *(lights off)*

The Light Comes   John 1:1-14; 8:12; 9:45; 11:9-10; 12:35-36; 12:44-48; 3:18-20

Hymn   "Were You There When They Crucified My Lord?" (vv. 3 and 4)

Men: Then the Roman soldiers with their commanding officer and the Jewish guards arrested Jesus, tied him up, and took him first to Annas. He was the father-in-law of Caiaphas, who was the high priest that year. It was Caiaphas who had advised the Jewish authorities that it was better that one man should die for all the people (John 18:12-14).

Women: Early in the morning, Jesus was taken from Caiaphas' house to the governor's palace.... Then Pilate took Jesus and had him whipped. The soldiers made a crown of thorny branches and put it on his head; then they put a purple robe on him and came to him and said, "Long live the King of the Jews!" and they went up and slapped him.... Then Pilate handed Jesus over to them to be crucified (John 18:28; 19:1-3, 16a).

All: So they took charge of Jesus. He went out, carrying his cross, and came to "The Place of the Skull," as it is called. (In Hebrew it is called "Golgotha.") There they crucified him, and they also crucified two other men, one on each side, with Jesus between them (John 19:16b-18). *(Silence)*

Optional Choral Anthem   "For God So Loved The World"

First Word
Jesus said, "Forgive them, Father! They don't know what they are doing" (Luke 23:34a).

All: Father, your Word says that you pity me the way a father pities his children. You know what I am made of; you remember that I am dust. Forgive me, Father, I truly don't know the full extent of anything I do (Psalm 103:13) *(silence)*

Second Word

"I promise you that today you will be in paradise with me" (Luke 23:39-43).

All: Thank you, Father, that it is never too late for me to cry out to you and to be accepted fully by you. Forgive me for the times I am too proud to admit my sin. Help me to turn to you. *(silence)*

Third Word

"He is your son." ... "She is your mother" (John 19:25-27).

All: In the middle of all your suffering, you thought of others. Forgive me, Jesus, for being so wrapped up in myself and my concerns that I ignore those around me. *(silence)*

Fourth Word

"*Eli, Eli lema sabachthani?*" which means, "My God, my God, why did you abandon me?" (Matthew 27:45-46).

All: Jesus, your word says that you know completely and totally what it is like to be a human being. You know — more than I do — what abandonment feels like. Thank you for becoming a human being, for living on this earth, and for dying a real death. *(silence)*

Fifth Word

"I am thirsty" (John 19:28).

Women: You promise to give us living water

Men: yet you thirsted.

All: And when you said you were thirsty, they gave you — the creator of all — cheap wine ... vinegar to drink. You thirst for me, and I offer you — my creator, my redeemer, my life — cheap wine ... vinegar. *(silence)*

Sixth Word

"It is finished" (John 19:30). *(silence)*

Seventh Word

"Father! In your hands I place my spirit!" (John 23:44-45).

Depart in silence

Sing To The Lord
A New Song

Easter Sunrise Service

Howard Eshbaugh

Sing To The Lord A New Song

Easter Sunrise Service

Call To Worship

Leader: Praise the Lord, all nations.

People: Christ died for our sins.

Leader: Extol him, all peoples.

People: Christ was buried but was raised from the dead.

Leader: For great is his steadfast love toward us.

People: In love God gave his Son.

Leader: The faithfulness of the Lord endures forever.

People: God's faithfulness has been shown to us in Christ.

All: Praise the Lord.

Prayer *(Unison)*

Father God, we come together on this morning to remember the resurrection of Jesus Christ. Through your written Word and through your Spirit, enable us to experience what happened on that first Easter morning and what it means to us. Amen.

Hymn

(Psalm 98:1-3 is to be sung antiphonally. If desired, a hymn suitable for Easter may be substituted.)

Leader: Sing to the Lord.

People: Sing to the Lord a new song.

Leader: His right hand and his holy arm have gotten him victory.

People: Victory.

Leader: The Lord has made known his victory.

People: Victory.

Leader: God has revealed this vindication.

People: Victory.

Leader: God has remembered his steadfast love and faithfulness to the house of Israel.

People: Victory.

Leader: All the ends of the earth have seen the victory of our God.

People: Victory.

All: Amen.

Litany   Philippians 2:5-11

Leader: Philippians 2:5-11 is an early Christian hymn. It has been described as the "gospel in a nutshell." It tells of the incarnation, ministry, death, and resurrection of Jesus Christ. In the services on Maundy Thursday and Good Friday, only portions of this passage were used. On this Easter day, the entire passage is used. The response is 2 Corinthians 8:9 which tells of the humility and service of Jesus Christ.

Leader:	Have this mind among yourselves, which you have in Christ Jesus.
People:	**For you know the grace of our Lord Jesus Christ, that though he was rich, yet for your sake he became poor, so that by his poverty you might become rich.**
Leader:	Who though he was in the form of God did not count equality with God a thing to be grasped.
People:	**For you know the grace of our Lord Jesus Christ, that though he was rich, yet for your sake he became poor, so that by his poverty you might become rich.**
Leader:	But he emptied himself, taking the form of a servant, being born in the likeness of men.
People:	**For you know the grace of our Lord Jesus Christ, that though he was rich, yet for your sake he became poor, so that by his poverty you might become rich.**
Leader:	And being found in human form, he humbled himself and became obedient unto death, even death on a cross.
People:	**For you know the grace of our Lord Jesus Christ, that though he was rich, yet for your sake he became poor, so that by his poverty you might become rich.**
Leader:	Therefore, God has highly exalted him and bestowed on him the name which is above every name.
People:	**For you know the grace of our Lord Jesus Christ, that though he was rich, yet for your sake he became poor, so that by his poverty you might become rich.**
Leader:	That at the name of Jesus every knee should bow, in heaven and on earth and under the earth, and every tongue confess that Jesus Christ is Lord, to the glory of God the Father.
People:	**For you know the grace of our Lord Jesus Christ, that though he was rich, yet for your sake he became poor, so that by his poverty you might become rich.**
All:	**Amen.**

Scripture
Luke 24:1-52

(The readers necessary for this reading are Narrator, Angel, Jesus, Cleopas, and Disciples.)

Narrator: But on the first day of the week, at early dawn, they went to the tomb, taking the spices which they had prepared. And they found the stone rolled away from the tomb, but when they went in, they did not find the body. While they were perplexed about this, behold, two men stood by them in dazzling apparel; and as they were frightened and bowed their faces to the ground, the men said to them,

Angel: "Why do you seek the living among the dead? Remember how he told you, while he was still in Galilee, that the Son of Man must be delivered into the hands of sinful men, and be crucified, and on the third day rise."

Narrator: And they remembered his words, and returning from the tomb they told all this to the eleven and to all the rest. Now it was Mary Magdalene and Joanna and Mary the mother of James and the other women with them who told this to the apostles, but these words seem to them an idle talk, and they did not believe them. That very day two of them were going to a village named Emmaus, about seven miles from Jerusalem, and talking with each other about all these things that had happened. While they were talking and discussing together, Jesus himself drew near and went with them. But their eyes were kept from recognizing him. And he said to them,

Jesus: "What is this conversation which you are holding with each other as you walk?"

Narrator: Then one of them, named Cleopas, answered him,

Cleopas: "Are you the only visitor to Jerusalem who does not know the things that have happened there in these days?"

Narrator: And he said to them,

Jesus: "What things?"

Narrator: And they said to him,

Cleopas: "Concerning Jesus of Nazareth, who was a prophet mighty in deed and word before God and all the people, and how our chief priests and rulers delivered him up to be condemned to death and crucified him. But we had hoped that he was the one to redeem Israel. Yes, and besides all this, it is now the third day since this happened. Moreover, some women of our company amazed us, they were at the tomb early in the morning and did not find his body, and they came back saying that they had even seen a vision of angels, who said that he was alive. Some of those who were with us went to the tomb, and found it just as the women had said; but him they did not see."

Narrator: And he said to them,

Jesus: "O foolish men, and slow of heart to believe all that the prophets have spoken! Was it not necessary that the Christ should suffer these things and enter into his glory?"

Narrator: And beginning with Moses and all the prophets, he interpreted to them in all the scriptures the things concerning himself. So they drew near to the village to which they were going; and he made as though he would go further, but they constrained him, saying,

Cleopas: "Stay with us, for it is toward evening and the day is now far spent."

Narrator: So he went in to stay with them. When he was at table with them, he took the bread and blessed, and broke it, and gave it to them. And their eyes were opened and they recognized him; and he vanished out of their sight. They said to each other,

Cleopas: "Did not our hearts burn with us while he talked to us on the road, while he opened us to the scriptures?"

Narrator: And they rose that same hour and returned to Jerusalem; and they found the eleven gathered together and those who were with them, who said,

Disciples: "The Lord has risen indeed, and has appeared to Simon!"

Narrator: Then they told what had happened on the road, and how he was known to them in the breaking of the bread. As they were saying this, Jesus himself stood among them. But they were startled and frightened, and supposed that they saw a spirit. And he said to them,

Jesus: "Why are you troubled, and why do questionings rise in your hearts? See my hands and feet, that it is I myself; handle me, and see; for a spirit has not flesh and bones as you see that I have."

Narrator: And while they still disbelieved for joy, and wondered, he said to them,

Jesus: "Have you anything to eat?"

Narrator: They gave him a piece of boiled fish, and he took it and ate before them. Then he said to them,

Jesus: "These are my words which I spoke to you, while I was still with you, that everything written about me in the law of Moses and the prophets and the psalms must be fulfilled."

Narrator: Then he opened their minds to understand the scriptures, and said to them,

Jesus: "Thus it is written, that the Christ should suffer and on the third day rise from the dead, and that repentance and forgiveness of sins should be preached in his name to all nations, beginning from Jerusalem. You are witness to these things. And behold, I send the promise of my Father upon you; but stay in the city, until you are clothed with power from on high."

Narrator: Then he led them out as far as Bethany, and lifting up his hands, he blessed them. While he blessed them, he parted from them. And they returned to Jerusalem with great joy, and were continually in the temple blessing God.

The Fish Meal
(At this time, let each person be given a fish-shaped cracker. These are available in most grocery stores. If a meal is to be served after the worship service, celebrate the Fish Meal at the table.)

Leader: This fish cracker can symbolize many things:

1. Jesus called disciples who were fishers. They were told they would become fishers of men.
2. A fish was the first food eaten by the risen Christ.
3. In John's gospel, the risen Jesus directs the disciples to a vast, symbolic (153) catch of fish. He later eats fish with them.
4. The fish is a symbol of Jesus Christ. The Greek word for "fish" is *ichthus.*
   The I stands for Jesus — Jesus
   The CH stands for Christos — Christ
   The TH for Theos — God
   The U for Huios — Son
   The S for Soter — Savior

This is the fish creed — Jesus Christ, God's Son, Savior. Let us affirm our faith by this creed and then eat the fish cracker. Jesus Christ, God's Son, Savior. Amen. *(eats cracker)*

Prayer

Father God, we thank you for the victory of the first Easter. As we remember this victory over sin and death, open our hearts that it may be part of our lives. Amen.

Hymn

(1 Corinthians 15:3-6 may be sung antiphonally. If desired, a hymn suitable for Easter may be substituted.)

Leader: 1 Corinthians 15:3-6 is a creedal affirmation about Jesus Christ. It is an announcement of the good news.

People: **Hear the good news, the good news**

Leader: The good news which you received, the good news in which you stand, and the good news by which your sins are saved.

People: **Christ died for our sins.**

Leader: This is according to scripture.

People: **He was buried**

Leader: But on the third day he was raised. This also is according to scripture. He appeared to Peter.

People: **To Peter.**

Leader: He appeared to the twelve.

People: **To Peter, to the twelve.**

Leader: He appeared to 500 others.

People: **To Peter, to the twelve, to 500 others.**

Leader: This is the good news, the good news.

People: **Christ died for our sins. Christ is raised from the dead.**

All: **Amen.**

Benediction

He Is Risen Indeed!

Easter Sunrise Worship Service

William Luoma

He Is Risen Indeed!

Introduction

There is one morning in the year when churches can get away with scheduling worship at a very early hour. That is Easter morning, of course! Some people will be there because they want to make the resurrection of Christ a reality in their lives. Others will come because their teenagers are in the youth group that is serving breakfast after the service. But whatever the motivation, it is a unique opportunity for a meaningful worship experience.

A sunrise service can be scheduled at one of the usual times: 6 a.m. or 6:30 a.m.; but some like to schedule it at whatever actual time the weather bureau predicts the sun will rise. It could be 6:13 a.m. or 6:27 a.m.

The entire service may be held outdoors. Select a site where the morning sun will be visible. If a site other than the church grounds is preferred, consider such locations as a nearby park, a dock, lakeshore, a cemetery, a hill, an outdoor amphitheater, or someone's farm.

If it is preferred to hold the service in the church, the congregation may assemble outside the building to begin the service, and proceed into the sanctuary after the psalm. The procession may include an Easter banner, a crucifer, lay readers, and minister. Some may want to use balloons or colorful streamers. Make it joyful! It's a celebration of a victory!

Lay participation is encouraged for responsive readings and the lessons.

He Is Risen Indeed!

Worship Service

Invocation

Leader: Christ is risen!

People: He is risen indeed!

Leader: Christ is alive! Christ is among us!

People: He lives, all glory to his name!

Leader: He said, "I am the resurrection and the life, he who believes in me, though he die, yet shall he live;

People: And whoever lives and believes in me shall never die."

Leader: Do you believe this?

People: Yes, Lord. I believe that you are the Christ, the Son of God, he who is coming into the world.

Leader: Thanks be to God who gives us the victory through our Lord Jesus Christ!

All: We greet the risen Lord, in the name of the Father, and of the Son, and of the Holy Spirit. Amen.

Hymn   "I Know That My Redeemer Lives!"

Prayer

Gracious God, we have come to celebrate the resurrection of your Son, Jesus Christ, from the dead. You sent him to us out of love. You raised him that we might have hope. Today we join with your people throughout the world to praise you and to give thanks for the new life we have in Jesus Christ, our Lord. Amen.

Psalm   Psalm 118:1-6, 15-24

Leader: Give thanks to the Lord, because he is good, and his love is eternal.

People: Let the people of Israel say, "His love is eternal."

Leader: Let the priests of God say, "His love is eternal."

People: Let all who worship him say, "His love is eternal."

Leader: In my distress I called to the Lord; he answered me and set me free.

People: The Lord is with me, I will not be afraid; what can anyone do to me?

Leader: Listen to the glad shouts of victory in the tents of God's people: "The Lord's almighty power has done it!"

People: His power has brought us victory; his mighty power in battle!

Leader: I will not die; instead, I will live and proclaim what the Lord has done.

People: He has punished me severely, but he has not let me die.

Leader: Open to me the gates of the temple; I will go in and give thanks to the Lord!

People: This is the gate of the Lord; only then righteous can come in.

Leader: I praise you, Lord, because you heard me, because you have given me victory.

People: **The stone which the builders rejected as worthless turned out to be the most important of all.**

Leader: This was done by the Lord; what a wonderful sight it is!

People: **This is the day of the Lord's victory; let us be happy, let us celebrate!**

Processional Hymn   "Jesus Christ Is Risen Today" or "Beautiful Savior"

First Lesson   Jonah 2:1-10

Reader: When Jesus was asked for a sign, he said no sign would be given except the sign of the prophet Jonah. He compared Jonah's experience in the fish to his own death. This is Jonah's prayer from within the fish. *(reads Jonah 2:1-10)*

Second Lesson   2 Corinthians 4:16—5:10

Reader: Saint Paul compares our limited and troublesome span of life to God's promise of eternal glory. We have this hope because of our faith. *(reads 2 Corinthians 4:16—5:19)*

Gospel   Luke 24:1-12

Reader: Luke's gospel describes the women at the tomb, who were the first ones to receive the news of the resurrection. *(reads Luke 24:1-12)*

Message

Statement Of Faith

The good news has come in Jesus Christ. He is the sign of the Father's love for us. He reveals to us that we are the children of God. He went about bringing joy to life. He gave himself, as he gave the fish to the poor, and as he provided bread and wine for his friends. He suffered for us and overcame death.

We, therefore, proclaim his death for us every time we gather. We proclaim his resurrection as we stand with other humans. We expect his return as we work for the world of tomorrow.

We know that we have received his gifts and that we are his church. In the newness of the spirit of this day, and with the grace of the sacrament made ours, we will live as the church for others. May it ever be so.

Share The Peace Of Christ With One Another

(Worshipers may greet one another with the words, "The peace of the Lord be with you," then respond, "And also with you.")

Hymn   "Break Now The Bread Of Life"
or "Let Us Break Bread Together On Our Knees"

The Holy Communion

Leader: The Lord be with you.

People: **And also with you.**

Leader: Lift up your hearts.

People:	**We lift them up to the Lord.**
Leader:	Let us give thanks to the Lord our God.
People:	**It is right to give him thanks and praise!**
Leader:	In the night in which he was betrayed, our Lord Jesus took bread, gave thanks, and broke it, and gave it to his disciples, saying, "Take and eat, this is my body, given for you."
People:	**We do this in remembrance of him.**
Leader:	Again, after supper, he took the cup, gave thanks, and gave it for all to drink, saying, "This cup is the new covenant in my blood, shed for you and for all people for the forgiveness of sin."
People:	**We do this in remembrance of him.**
All:	**Our Father in heaven, hallowed be your name; your kingdom come, your will be done, on earth as in heaven. Give us today our daily bread. Forgive us our sins as we forgive those who sin against us. Save us from the time of trial and deliver us from evil; for the kingdom, the power, and the glory are yours, now and forever. Amen.**

(*Worshipers receive the elements of communion.*)

Prayer

Gracious Lord, we give thanks for you have nourished us at your table, assured us of your love, and strengthened us to walk in faith. Go with us as we go our separate ways, filled with your Spirit, for you have revealed yourself to us in the breaking of the bread. In Christ's name we ask. Amen.

Blessing

May the blessing of the eternal God be upon us, and upon our loved ones: His light to guide us, his presence to strengthen us, his love to unite us, now and always. Amen.

Hymn   "I Serve A Risen Savior"

The Big Secret

Easter Monologue

Michelle Griep

The Big Secret

Easter Monologue

Notes

This Easter monologue is an interpretation of Matthew 26:57-50.

Scene

A teenage girl (or young looking woman) enters to center stage.

Stage Setting

Empty — no special needs

I have a secret — a big secret. If my master finds out, I'll be in trouble for sure, but I'm bursting to tell. In fact, there's someone I'm looking for who needs to hear this, but I might as well tell you first.

The last few days have been kind of crazy around here. A couple of nights ago, my master, that's Lord Caiaphas, had all the servants of his house awakened late into the fourth watch.

Guards, soldiers, temple leaders, men were everywhere, and lots of them. At first I didn't know what was going on. Raised voices and angry words spilled out into the courtyard where I rushed to fill empty goblets.

I heard the guards placing bets on what would happen to the man inside. "Jesus" they called him. I'd heard that name many times. My master hates him.

Near the fire, warming his hands, a man stood who held no cup. I started to bring him one, but stopped. Something about him reminded me of the man inside. Strands of brown curls and dark eyes reflecting the flames labeled him as Jewish as any of the others gathered there that night. I squinted and thought real hard, then I knew. His robe. A worn, homespun robe. I knew where that fabric came from.

"Hey, you're from Galilee. You're one of his friends. Why aren't you in there with him?"

When he looked at me, I swallowed in fear. That kind of rage usually meant a beating. He didn't hit me, but he did yell. I've been cursed at before, but never like that. I couldn't stop the hot tears of shame and embarrassment, so I ran to the shadows.

That's when I saw the guards shove Jesus into the courtyard. I'd seen him before at the temple, but this time I almost didn't recognize him.

Stripped nearly naked, they spat on him and took turns striking him until he fell. I heard the force grind the flesh of his knees into the gravel. His gentle brown eyes winced in pain, but he didn't cry out.

The things they said, the awful names they called him, made me forget about what had been said to me. I wanted to stop it, to run and protect him, but I didn't. What could I do? I'm only a girl, and a slave at that.

111

Everyone turned on him. Not one defended him. No one. He was all alone against the evil.

As soon as I could get away the next day, I decided I'd find this man, Jesus, and be his friend. I'd bring him a honeycake and a small skin of wine. I could patch up those bruises of his and ... then I found out.

He died.

I felt sick.

Later that night, lying on my pallet, I had a great idea. Maybe I could still be his friend by honoring his death. If I asked around, I'd find his tomb and bring him respect even if no one else did.

That's where the big secret comes in. I did find out. I even went there today. I thought I'd get there early but on my way, three women came rushing down the path. One of them grabbed my shoulders and smiled right into my face.

"He's alive girl. He's alive! Tell everyone!"

They rushed off leaving me staring after their swishing robes. I didn't know what to think. Not until I got to the tomb and saw it empty. How could that be? I didn't understand, and I still don't really, but I believe what that man at the tomb told me. He said Jesus wasn't dead, but alive. And you know, he had the same gentle brown eyes.

So, now you know. I'm on my way to tell everyone but especially that man that yelled at me the other night. I think he'd want to know that there's still a chance to be Jesus' friend.

Contributors

Anne W. Anderson is a freelance writer, photojournalist, and speaker who answers the question, "What denomination are you?" with "I am a Christian." She has been strongly influenced by Episcopalians, Presbyterians, Baptists, Catholics, Messianic Jews, and the people at Aldersgate United Methodist Church in Seminole, Florida, where she serves as drama director, teaches Sunday school, and sings in the choir. She has written other dramas, which are included in *Destination: Bethlehem* (CSS, 2004). Having attended the University of California, Irvine, the University of Wyoming, and St. Petersburg Junior College (A.A., 1992), she is working toward her B.A. in creative writing from Eckerd College, St. Petersburg, Florida.

Lynne Cragg is a private music teacher who serves as the accompanist for several elementary and middle school choirs in Parker, Colorado. She is a graduate of The King's College, New York, New York, with a degree in elementary education, and is currently working on her master's degree in counseling at Capella University. She is active in women's ministries, music ministries, and as a Bible teacher at Parker Evangelical Presbyterian Church.

Howard Eshbaugh (1931-1999) was Pastor Emeritus of First Presbyterian Church of Glendale, Ohio. He had also served at Florence Presbyterian Church in Florence, Pennsylvania, and Hillcrest United Presbyterian Church in Burgettstown, Pennsylvania. A graduate of Grove City College, Western Theological Seminary, and Pittsburgh Seminary, he received his Ph.D. in New Testament and Christian origins from Case Western Reserve University. He was the author of *Hearing The Word* (CSS, 1984).

Michelle Griep has four children and wears her stay-at-home mom badge with pride. She has homeschooled for the past fourteen years and in her spare time is a freelance author, typographer, and copywriter. She received her A.A. from Minneapolis Community College. She attends Bethlehem Baptist Church and is actively involved in REACH (Reaching for Excellence in Academics through Christian Homeschooling). A member of Minnesota Christian Writers Guild and American Christian Fiction Writers, she has written for several newspapers and ezines.

Leonard V. Kalkwarf is a retired minister of the Reformed Church in America, having served Reformed congregations in upstate New York, Long Island, Pennsylvania, an international congregation in Kuwait, and a Presbyterian church near Philadelphia, Pennsylvania. He holds an M.A. from New York University, an S.T.M. from the Lutheran Theological Seminary in Philadelphia, and a D.Min from Princeton Seminary. A past president of the General Synod of the Reformed Church in America, he has written catechism books (The Half Moon Press), as well as *An Historical Sketch of The First Reformed Dutch Church of The City and Vicinity of Philadelphia* (private publisher, 1960).

William Luomo is a retired pastor who served churches in Bowling Green, Port Clinton, and Logan, Ohio. He is a graduate of Trinity Lutheran Seminary and Capital University in Columbus, Ohio. He and his wife, Lois, are the parents of three adult children. He is the author of *God So Loved The World — Worship Services For Ash Wednesday and Holy Week* (CSS, 1986) and devotional series for *Christ in Our Home* and *My Devotions*.

Pamela D. Williams has been a pastor's wife for thirty years. A mother and grandmother, she has a B.A. in English from Shipensburg University. She is actively involved in all the ministries at Everett United Methodist Church in Everett, Pennsylvania. A freelance writer, she has had stories published in a variety of publications, including *Decision, Upper Room*, and *Chicken Soup for the Soul: Stories for a Better World*.

Janice Bennett Wyatt (1919-2005) served in the youth and Christian education departments in the United Church of Christ in Des Moines, Iowa; Worcester, Massachusetts; Greenbelt, Maryland; Glen Ridge, New Jersey; and Jefferson, Maryland. She was a graduate of New Jersey State College and received her M.A. from Garrett Seminary in Evanston, Illinois. She was the author of *Come, Let Us Adore Him* (CSS, 1992).